TILLICH

A Brief Overview
of the Life and Writings
of Paul Tillich

Daniel J. Peterson

Lutheran University Press
Minneapolis, Minnesota

TILLICH
A Brief Overview of the
Life and Writings of Paul Tillich
by Daniel J. Peterson

Theology for Life Series, Albert Anderson editor

Cover and interior design: Karen Walhof

Library of Congress Cataloging-in-Publication Data

Peterson, Daniel J., 1972-
  TILLICH : A Brief Overview of the Life and Writings of Paul Til-
lich / Daniel J. Peterson.
      pages cm
  ISBN-13: 978-1-932688-86-3 (alk. paper)
  ISBN-10: 1-932688-86-2 (alk. paper)
  1. Tillich, Paul, 1886-1965. I. Title.
  BX4827.T53P39 2013
  230.092--dc23
                                    2013010273

Lutheran University Press, PO Box 390759, Minneapolis, MN 55439
www.lutheranupress.org
Manufactured in the United States of America

DEDICATION

To my mentors, Lutheran and Jesuit,
who have encouraged me in my questioning
and walked with me in my search for meaning—
especially Rev. Steve Hanson, the Rev. Dr. Timothy Lull,
the Rev. Dr. John H. Elliott, the Rev. Dwane Michael,
the Rev. John Vaswig, Vernon Ruland, SJ,
and John Foster, SJ

CONTENTS

FOREWORD

Since his death in 1965, Paul Tillich has continued to interest and excite the minds and hearts of both scholars and religious seekers. Born in Germany in 1886, young Paulus, as he was called in German, was destined to a career as an academic scholar and an ordained minister in his church. At the age of twenty-eight, he was summoned to a chaplaincy in the German army during World War I, an event that changed his life forever. After the war, his conservative religious values gave way to the bohemian life style of Germany in the 1920s; his theology and philosophy were no longer centered on the church but on broader cultural and social issues; his politics became socialist. The Nazi government forced him into exile in 1933. Without knowing a word of the English language, bereft of his friends and his homeland, he came to New York City with his wife and daughter to teach at Union Theological Seminary as a visiting professor. In little more than a quarter of a century, he appeared on the cover of *Time* magazine in 1959 and was proclaimed America's "foremost Protestant thinker."

The genius of Paul Tillich's writings is that they are profound, comprehensive, and synthetic, yet accessible, particularly in his sermons and popular writings, to the religious seeker and non-specialist. Although primarily theological and philosophical, his works cross many disciplines: culture, history, politics, art and architecture, the sciences, and psychology. Tillich was as at home corresponding with Martin Buber, the great Jewish thinker, as he was with Albert Einstein, the most prominent scientist of his era. He was at home in Riverside Church, preaching sermons that moved people's souls; he was also at home in Madison Square Garden during World War

II, addressing rallies to support the Jewish émigrés who were victims of the Nazis. And he was just as comfortable speaking at the Metropolitan Museum of Art or the Art Institute of Chicago, or dialoguing with a group of psychologists and psychoanalysts, as he was with academics in his own field.

While a distinguished scholar and thinker, Tillich wrote in a manner that spoke to anyone seeking answers to the ultimate questions of life. He gave people a new language about God, the world, and themselves; he offered those who had left the churches a broader view of what it means to be religious, what it means to find the sacred in the emptiness of modern culture, when the foundations of belief are truly shaken. Although a Lutheran, Tillich was never fully accepted by the Lutheran churches in the United States. He stood in the vestibule of the churches—on the boundary between church and world, he writes. He was a man often more at home in secular culture, with the masses of those who had left their faith and hope behind, than in the pews.

What has long been needed is a book on Tillich for the non-specialist, for someone who may be reading a volume of Tillich's sermons, his writings on religion after World War I, or his important publications of the 1950s such as *The Courage to Be* or *Dynamics of Faith*. Daniel Peterson has written such a book, and it is a pleasure and honor for me to introduce it to you. Professor Peterson presents the reader to Tillich both historically and thematically. His exploration of Tillich's German period (1886–1933) cogently links the events in Tillich's life to the development of his thought, especially the profound change that took place during his chaplaincy years, his relationship to the thought of Karl Barth, and the evolution of his idea of history from the idealism of Hegel to history filled with moments of *kairos*, those unpredictable special times that call for a decision.

Peterson continues Tillich's journey to America (1933–1965), through his two decades at Union Theological Seminary, his university professorship at Harvard in the late 1950s, and his death in Chicago in 1965. Many who heard his sermons and read his books considered him a savior. Conservatives, on the other hand, believed he was a very dangerous man both theologically and politically. Traditional Americans were not used to hearing a theologian proclaiming that God does not "exist," or that there was a "God above God"! Ideology aside, Peterson wisely emphasizes the existential impact of Tillich on the broader culture—how Tillich changed lives, including his own. Tillich taught him, as he says, "that one did not have to sacrifice one's mind to be a Christian." Indeed, doubt is an essential part of faith. Although he was thinker in the same company of a few other great minds of the twentieth century, Peterson notes that "Tillich was able to communicate his highly abstract ideas in a language much more concrete than his own to a culture more practical than his own."

Thematically, Peterson explores those topics uniquely identified with Tillich's thought: meaning, faith, symbols, God, courage, and Christ. In each area, Peterson seamlessly weaves together his own thought along with current Tillich scholarship on each topic. Indeed, his grasp of the scholarly literature is impressive, judiciously citing both those who agree with Tillich and those who dissent. Yet, the author is not interested in scholarly debate. He is primarily a teacher, and each theme is explored systematically, as one might do in a classroom: Tillich's intellectual ancestry, his own understanding and conceptual framework, and the influence of his ideas—pro or con—on thinkers who followed him. Peterson's treatment of God as "being-itself," the problem with the idea of the "existence" of God, the debate over God as personal or impersonal, is a simple yet profound *tour de force* of one of the most historically rich and complex questions in all of theology. In his concluding chapter, Peterson summarizes Tillich's contributions and his widespread influence on the methodology, theology, and spirituality in the last half of the twentieth century, including women theologians influenced by his system, the developing field of eco-theology, and postmodern thought. In some afterthoughts, Peterson includes a helpful paragraph for anyone encountering Tillich's writings for the first time.

Professor Daniel Peterson's book fills an important gap in Tillich scholarship: It is a splendid primer on all things Tillich for the beginning reader. Those well acquainted with Tillich writings, however, will also find this book stimulating and nourishing. As someone who has taught Paul Tillich to undergraduates for many years, I have long wanted to publish an introduction to Tillich that was accessible to undergraduates and the non-specialist reader. Professor Peterson has accomplished what I have failed to do; he has written the book that I always wanted to write myself. I look forward to using this book in my next undergraduate class on Tillich. This work is succinct, accurate, and well researched. It offers the reader a clear vision of Tillich's own vast vision, and is an essential guide to those embarking on the grand adventure of reading Paul Tillich today.

Frederick J. Parrella
Santa Clara University
18 February 2013

PREFACE

What does the Christian faith have to say to people who wonder about its teachings? Can it speak in a credible and intelligent way to those who find themselves seeking answers to questions including whether God is real or why there is so much suffering in the world? Is it compatible with science, questioning, and doubt? While critics might understandably answer in the negative to these questions by insisting that the Christian faith lacks empirical evidence or sound reasoning to support its claims, the truth is that compelling options do exist concerning what Christians teach and believe; the problem is that many people do not know about them.

The present volume offers one such option by introducing readers to the life and work of Paul Tillich, a theologian (i.e., someone who explores faith using reason) who has become virtually unknown outside of academic circles since his death in 1965. Though effort has been made recently to recover Tillich's theology for a larger audience, a number of authors do so by retracing the arc of his entire theological "system" in compelling but sometimes overwhelming ways, at least to those who are unfamiliar with his thought. What we need—and what I hope to provide in the pages that follow—is an overview of Tillich's theology in smaller, bite-sized fragments that will make the journey into his thought-world easier for newcomers who are curious to learn more but who may not speak the technical language that theologians (like Tillich himself) often use.

My own journey into Tillich's thought-world began when I was in college. During that time I asked a lot of questions about my faith tradition. Seeking answers, I took several courses in religion, deciding eventually to minor in the subject. About a year into the minor one of my professors assigned Tillich's *Dynamics of Faith*, a profound little book that Tillich wrote mid-century as an attempt to make his theology more accessible. In this work Tillich directly addresses the "problem" of faith and doubt. While many assume the two are antithetical, he maintains that serious doubt (as distinct from lazy or indifferent cynicism) actually confirms faith since it implies a deeper thirst and concern for that about which one is raising questions. This insight was for me revolutionary. Here one of the greatest theologians of the twentieth century had named and confirmed my experience; here a theologian had finally, as Martin Luther would say, "called a thing what it is."

What Tillich taught me, in short, was that one did not have to sacrifice one's mind to be a Christian. I could acknowledge my doubt fully and openly for the first time as part of my faith; I could see doubt as a corollary to faith understood not as a belief with little or no evidence but as an attitude of trust in something greater, something beyond ourselves, something ultimate—the name of which Christians (and Jews and Muslims) call God. Over the years I have returned again and again to Tillich's explanation of faith, always grateful for the fact that he opened the door to a deeper way of being Christian and with it a more "dynamic" understanding of faith. To those who desire the same kind of faith along with a type of Christianity open to science, wonder, questioning and reflection, Tillich can be a terrific resource, especially at a time when it seems like the only option that exists is dogmatism or certainty in matters of religion.

As a native of Germany, Tillich knew from his experience of nationalism the danger of faith when it is unable to acknowledge and incorporate the element of uncertainty. Pledging allegiance to the absolute authority of the state (i.e., placing one's complete faith in the god of the nation) cost millions of people in Germany and throughout Europe their lives. Those like Tillich who criticized the authority and actions of the state were considered traitors. Doubt or questioning in any form was unacceptable. We can see the same phenomenon, though obviously on a lesser scale, when it comes to religious faith that vehemently rejects doubt: by failing to appropriate doubt as part of what Tillich would call his "ultimate concern," the "believer" becomes rigid. He represses the questions that seem to threaten his unconditional devotion to "God" or the Bible, failing to recognize the element of risk that necessarily accompanies faith and with it the possibility that something else might be the case. Those who remind the believer of the possibility that he could be wrong by raising questions about his faith become "enemies of the faith." They represent the doubt the believer was unable consciously to incorporate (Paul Tillich, *The Courage to Be* [hereafter, *CTB*], Yale University Press, 2000 [1952], p. 50).

The fact that repression of doubt could have such negative consequences was at least one of the reasons behind Tillich's conviction that, as he shared in a letter to a personal friend, it was his "mission to bring doubt to the faithful" (Rollo May, *Paulus: Tillich as Spiritual Teacher*, Saybrook Publishing Company, 1988, p. 71). He knew, as his colleague Reinhold Niebuhr would affirm, that a person's attempt to obscure his limited knowledge by identifying his finite perspective with the Absolute "is always prompted by the fear of meaninglessness" (*Reinhold Niebuhr: Theologian of Public Life*, ed. Larry Rasmussen, Fortress Press, 1991, p. 140). Yet Tillich also felt that his mission as a theologian was "to bring faith to the faithless" (May, op. cit., p. 71). Indeed, after moving from Germany to America in 1933, his main focus became that of reaching people for whom the Christian message had become irrelevant or without significance. As the theologian David Kelsey explains, Tillich's "principal goal was to make Christianity understandable and persuasive to religiously skeptical people, modern in culture and secular in sensibility" (*The Fabric of Paul Tillich's*

Theology, Yale University Press, p. 87). This involved translating the Christian message into language that would make sense to people whose worldview was informed less by Sunday School Christianity and more by science. While some considered him accordingly to be "the apostle to the intellectuals," Tillich was also read and heard by seekers unaffiliated with a college or university, many of whom felt assurance when he reminded them, as he does in one his sermons, that "in the depth of every serious doubt and every despair of truth, the passion for truth is still at work." Such doubt, he observes, constitutes a life "rich in God" (Paul Tillich, *The Eternal Now*, Charles Scribner's Sons, 1963, p. 40).

Times have obviously changed. Rarely do we hear popular ministers praise doubt as an element of faith. Instead, religion has largely become a reactionary force that sees doubt as a weakness and science as the enemy. On the other end of the spectrum, as the journalist and popular writer Gregg Easterbrook observes, "hard-hearted postmodernism assumes existence to lack meaning." Soon it becomes evident that "[i]n public debate, nihilism [the view that life has no ascertainable meaning] endlessly vies with fundamentalism. Each person who thinks about spiritual issues is expected to choose up sides, believing everything or nothing" (*Beside Still Waters: Searching for Meaning in an Age of Doubt*, William Morrow, 1998, p. viii). Where, then, do we turn? Might Tillich once again provide a third way between these extremes for people who, though rightly skeptical, find themselves asking seriously the question of truth and pondering its relation to faith? Tillich did this for me. Whether he can do this for others will ultimately be for you, the reader, to decide.

In the chapters ahead you will, if unfamiliar with Tillich's thought, encounter some conceptually challenging ideas. Be patient as you go. A fair portion of these ideas may become clearer as you proceed. Others, as you will see in chapters six and seven when I discuss Tillich's understanding of God, may require a second reading. That said, I have endeavored as much as possible either to explain the technical terminology that Tillich employs or to avoid it for the sake of introducing his thought in general terms. For readers more familiar with Tillich's work, this will explain the absence of certain vocabulary, including his discussion of concepts like "theonomy" or the "ontological elements" in the first volume of his *Systematic Theology*, all of which is important but (in my judgment) not essential for grasping the basic aspects of Tillich's thought. Readers who are curious to explore Tillich's theology beyond what I cover in the present work will find resources and suggestions for doing so at the end of the volume.

A final issue that may be challenging to some readers concerns Tillich's exclusively masculine language for human beings. Tillich was a product of his time. While he mostly uses the male pronoun in reference to humanity, he intends (like we all do when we sometimes employ the universal "man") to be inclusive. That said, in an effort to reflect the intention explicitly, I have consciously made the attempt in my summary of Tillich's perspective to alternate between male and female pronouns so as not to alienate any of my readers. When quoting Tillich, however, I have left the pronoun usage in its original form, whether he is talking about human beings or God. My hope is that those who are sensitive to the issue can overlook the minor brushstrokes of linguistic convention that Tillich inherited in order to see the "big picture" of God and all humanity that emerges on the canvas of his theology.

CHAPTER ONE

GERMANY

Paul Tillich was born in 1886 in Starzeddel, a small village that was in the eastern part of Germany which now belongs to Poland. At the age of four he moved with his family to Schön-fliess, a nearby provincial town where his father—a Lutheran pastor—took an appointment as the supervisor of other ministers in the region. Schönfliess left a deep impression on the young Tillich. Walls encircled the city which at its center had a Gothic church, giving the child a sense of living in a safe and "self-contained world" that was rich in cultural tradition. Eventually the town came to symbolize what Tillich describes as life in the nineteenth century. "Belonging to the nineteenth century implies life in relatively peaceful circumstances," he explains, "and recalls the highest flourishing of bourgeois [upper class] society in its productive grandeur" (*The Essential Tillich* [hereafter, *ET*], ed. F. Forrester Church, The University of Chicago Press, 1987, p. 250). While Tillich was also critical of the era, the stability he knew as a child was something about which he reminisced throughout adulthood; it was to him a Garden of Eden, life before the fall.

Life in this paradise afforded Tillich many opportunities to encounter and commune with nature. Every year he and his family traveled to the Baltic Sea where he would marvel at the vast and majestic expanse of the horizon at the water's edge. This, he says, was the annual experience that eventually gave rise to his sense of the infinite (i.e., God) as the limitless source or ocean of being from which all being emerges. The whole order of nature, in other words, became for Tillich "the finite expression of the infinite ground of all things" (*Ibid.*, p. 251), a transparency through which he could encounter God—not as a being who reigns from the *height* of the cosmos in heaven, but as the font or wellspring of being that resides at the *heart* of the cosmos as its core and ground (see Acts 17:28).

While Tillich's encounter with the infinite occurred through nature, the language he used to describe it came first from his father, a strict and devout man who subscribed to a dogmatic version of Lutheran Christianity. Tillich's relationship with his father was an uneasy one. As Mark K. Taylor observes in an introduction to Tillich's theology, "early tensions" between son and father grew worse until the former "wielded the very philosophy his father had taught him to love against the authoritarian pressure his father held over him" (Mark K. Taylor, "Introduction" in *Paul Tillich: Theologian of the Boundaries*, Fortress Press, 1991, p. 15). Eventually this would become fundamental to Tillich's way of doing theology: drawing from the Christian theological tradition he would challenge those who demanded submission to doctrine, pointing out their graceless desire to earn God's favor by sacrificing their intellects to ostensibly "sacred" authorities. Opposite his father, Tillich describes his mother as a generous and warm person. Unfortunately, she died of cancer when Tillich was 17. The tragedy of her death would never leave him.

Tillich drank deeply from the well of Lutheranism bequeathed to him by his father, particularly when it came to his understanding of God's relation to the world. His fundamental conviction that finite, material reality (i.e., the "stuff" of this world) abounds with the presence of God finds its precedent in a position taken by sixteenth century Lutherans in opposition to the views of John Calvin and his followers. Both parties agreed that human beings and all of nature have been "estranged" or separated from God, a condition symbolized by the fall of Adam from God's favor in Genesis 3. The Lutherans, however, insisted paradoxically that God simultaneously remains present in the world, much the way the power of healing can saturate even the deepest of wounds. To suggest otherwise, they argued, would be to deny the reality of the incarnation (the belief that God took human form in the person of Jesus), not to mention the transference of God's healing power to humanity through the flesh of Christ. The upshot of the debate was this: for the Lutherans the divine does not heal from a distance; the world can bear the healing presence of God.

Over time the debate between the Lutherans and the Calvinists resulted in a sharp distinction between the so-called *infra lutheranum* and the *extra calvinisticum*, the former affirming the real presence of God in nature and history, the latter denying God's presence in the world due to its immersion in sin. Tillich's contemporary and eventual rival, the theologian Karl Barth, took up and affirmed the *extra calvinisticum* with the publication of his commentary on Paul's Letter to the Romans in 1919 (revised edition, 1922), dividing the otherworldly holiness of God and the sinful state of humanity so sharply that no human effort—not even raising *the question* of God—could reorient people toward the divine. While Tillich agreed that salvation or spiritual healing could only come from God, he came to believe that for a theology to be truly "dialectical"—as Barth claimed his was—the human being should at least be able to raise the question of God. Otherwise, the Christian message and the answers it provides to the human predicament would be irrelevant. How, Tillich wondered, can a person receive a meaningful answer to a question he never asked?

Tillich's encounter with Barth as well as his debt to Luther and the Lutheran tradition will occupy us later in the chapters that follow, particularly as we consider more thoroughly his understanding of God. We will also examine the influence of two other Lutherans on Tillich—the philosopher Sören Kierkegaard and one of Tillich's teachers, the theologian Martin Kähler—when it comes to his view of faith and its relation to doubt. One thing, however, remains to be said here about

Barth: he offered a viewpoint against which Tillich would hone his own theological thinking. Indeed, Barth was the first of the two to arrive at a definitive theological position. In 1914 Barth watched in frustration as many of his former theology professors endorsed Kaiser Wilhelm II of Germany and his call for war. Barth interpreted their support as a capitulation to nationalism—one that revealed how easily their liberal Protestantism (which, he held, placed undue confidence in the ability of human reasoning and moral judgment at the expense of faith and trust in God) could be co-opted by the surrounding culture and its thirst for power. While Tillich came to a similar realization (though not as extreme, as we will show in a later chapter), he did so only *after* he enlisted in the German military.

Tillich entered the German army in 1914 at the age of 28. Now an ordained pastor of the Evangelical Church of the Prussian Union as well as the recipient of two doctoral degrees in theology and philosophy (the latter at the age of 24!), he became a chaplain. In a short time the newly-minted clergyman, one whose ministerial experience at that point was limited to eight months in a rural parish and a brief vicarage in Berlin, would participate in the longest and bloodiest conflict of the First World War—the Battle of Verdun. There he served for half a year as both "pastor and grave digger" (*Ibid.,* p. 16). What began as a decision to enter the army under the spell of German nationalism quickly transformed for the young chaplain into an experience of absolute terror. A letter to his father from the front lines consolidates an inventory of what must have been horrific images into just a few stammering words: "Hell rages around us. It's unimaginable" (*Ibid.,* p. 11). The superficial optimism that inspired Tillich and many other Germans of the time to join the army had now disappeared. The confidence in human potential that he and his other contemporaries inherited was now lost.

Tillich's experience of war changed everything, including his worldview. The widespread devastation he witnessed shattered the faith in historical progress he received from theologians and other thinkers who came before him in nineteenth century. One of the most influential of these thinkers was the philosopher G. W. F. Hegel. According to Hegel, God (the "Absolute Spirit" or "Absolute Idea") marches through history by means of the interplay of contrary forces that ultimately achieve resolution within time. This resolution occurs when the Idea—twisting, turning and colliding with itself through the opposing political, religious, and cultural movements of history—becomes aware of itself though philosophical, self-reflective human consciousness. A final merger of God with humanity constitutes the result of the process. Such a result was hardly apparent to Tillich after Verdun. History, he came to believe, is not the self-manifestation of the divine, as in Hegel's teaching, "but a series of unreconciled conflicts, threatening man with self-destruction" (Paul Tillich, *Systematic Theology,* vol. 2 [hereafter *ST*], The University of Chicago Press, 1957, p. 25). Twentieth century theology, freed from the naïve optimism of its forbears, had begun.

Tillich's new assessment of history as a "series of unreconciled conflicts" would sadly find its confirmation in what the Tillich scholar David Kelsey regards—after the theologian's experience on the front lines—as the second major turning-point in Tillich's life, namely, his confrontation with the emerging Nazi regime beginning in the late 1920s. By now Tillich had been a professor for nearly a decade as well as a participant in what historians generally regard as the wildly experimental post-war culture of the Weimar Republic. He taught at several universities, including one in Marburg where he was the colleague of Rudolf Bultmann (later to become a famous biblical scholar) and Martin Heidegger (one of the twentieth century's most important philosophers). Both of these men, especially Heidegger, would subsequently influence Tillich's thought and will thus merit our attention later. At this moment in Tillich's life, however, the question of Germany's political future was more pressing. Tillich devoted much of his mental energy therefore to developing a political system of thought that would eventually challenge the national socialism advocated by the Nazi party.

According to Wilhelm and Marion Pauck, two of Tillich's most trusted biographers, Tillich stood in opposition to the Nazi party from the beginning. He "detested everything for which the Nazis stood," they write, "and his growing anger, usually hidden beneath carefully worded theoretical statements, was aroused in public a number of times, causing him to explode and frightening his friends and his wife, who felt he was endangering himself" (Wilhelm and Marion Pauck, *Paul Tillich: His Life and Thought*, Harper & Row, 1989, p. 125f). Tillich's collision with the Nazis came to a head when he was the dean of the philosophical faculty at the University of Frankfurt in 1932. After fighting had erupted among students, those sympathetic to Nazism "rioted and beat up left-wing and Jewish students until blood flowed freely. In the classroom where he was lecturing, Tillich was suddenly thrown back into his World War I role of dragging the wounded and unconscious to safety" (*Ibid.*, p. 127). Infuriated, Tillich gave a speech shortly thereafter where he publicly denounced the Nazi students and called for their expulsion, defending the freedom of thought.

Tillich's demand for an expulsion did not go unheard by the Nazi party, only for them it was not the students who needed to be removed. By April of 1933 the Nazis banned Tillich and 1,683 other instructors from their teaching posts (*Ibid.*, p. 130). The publication of Tillich's *The Socialist Decision* in 1933 sealed his fate. There Tillich openly defied the party by endorsing the alternative of what he called "religious socialism," a move that put him in increasing danger. His closest friends accordingly began to express grave concerns about his safety. In May of that same year, he watched in horror as the Nazis burned his book along with hundreds of others. The war on "left-wing intellectuals, members of the Communist or Socialist parties, the politically suspect" and the Jews had begun (*Ibid*). Tillich had the "honor," as he would often later say, of being one of its first professional casualties.

The good news is that Tillich did not go without a fight. Perhaps the most direct and succinct attack Tillich waged on Nazism appears in a series of "Ten Theses" he wrote (he was Lutheran after all) where he dismisses "the paganism of the swastika" by appealing to what he would eventually label the Protestant Principle. Tillich based the Protestant Principle on Luther's criticism of the divine authority claimed by the medieval Catholic Church. Any person, group, political power or religious institution that takes the place of God by demanding unconditional and absolute allegiance (which for Luther was the Catholic Church of his time) must be recognized and challenged for what he or it is—an idol. Following this criterion, Tillich declared that the German church must confront the German nation with the charge of idolatry: "Protestantism must testify that the cross has broken and judged the 'holiness' of nation, race, blood, and power" (*Paul Tillich: Theologian of the Boundaries* [hereafter *PTTB*], ed. Mark K. Taylor, Fortress Press, 1991, p. 117). Those German Christians supportive of Nazism had violated the first of the Ten Commandments by replacing the Almighty with the Aryan. The Nazis dealt with such criticism swiftly, as noted above: they banned and burned *The Socialist Decision,* blacklisted Tillich, and dismissed his criticism as religious-political garbage.

What, then, could Tillich do? He was now jobless, past his mid-forties, married, and a father. His options were limited: at great risk to himself and his family he might stay and work in his homeland by going underground, or he could accept the invitation of Reinhold Niebuhr, a professor at Union Theological Seminary in New York who had become familiar with his work while recently in Germany, to join their faculty. Tillich vacillated. He knew little about American culture and had virtually no knowledge of English. There would be tremendous pangs of guilt should he leave; yet his death (as his close friends told him) was likely if he stayed. Would it be fair to his family to remain? While some critics would later begrudge him for what he was about to decide, anyone sympathetic to the burden of such decision-making can see in Tillich's case the predicament of choice at its most extreme. It was truly a matter of life and death.

After much wavering, Tillich finally decided to accept Niebuhr's invitation and depart for the United States. Hannah, his wife, was overjoyed. In the end it took the family nearly two months before they could leave, and in the process Tillich himself struggled with intense bouts of depression and anxiety. The Paucks describe the scene of his departure in unforgettable, almost cinematic terms: "It was a cold, rainy morning. At the station to see [Tillich and his family] off were their friends . . . and his sister Elisabeth and her husband Ehrard Seeberger. Tillich was strained, tense, quiet, almost desperate. He was more concerned about the fate of his Jewish friends than his own" (Pauck, op. cit., p. 138). Perhaps he wondered if he had made the right decision. Maybe the Nazi-terror would be short-lived. Maybe he could still be effective in the resistance if he stayed. Whatever might have gone through his mind, he and his family boarded a train for Hamburg, and from there a ship across stormy waves to a land of new possibilities. Tillich's time in Germany had come to its end.

CHAPTER TWO

AMERICA

The voyage across the churning waters of the Atlantic was a long one. Tillich spent much of his time on deck, telling his biographers years later that he never observed waves so high. In November of 1933 he and his family arrived in New York. A thick blanket of fog initially prevented their ship from docking. When it cleared, an open sky and "brilliant sunshine" (*Ibid.,* p. 140) welcomed Tillich as it has many other political refugees who have journeyed from distant countries seeking asylum in America. On shore several faculty from Columbia University, which had also indicated its desire to employ Tillich as a guest lecturer (and eventually did on occasion), were present to greet him. By the end of the day Tillich was in the company of Niebuhr who would become a lifelong advocate and friend as well as perhaps his closest and most important professional colleague. A new chapter had begun.

Naturally it would be tempting to depict the bright light of Tillich's first day in the United States as a symbol of the trouble-free life that was to follow. A vast distance now separated him from the gray skies of Nazi Germany. New possibilities glimmered on the American horizon. The truth of the matter, however, was that dark clouds of uncertainty still lingered overhead. The position Niebuhr arranged for him at Union was at first only temporary, one made possible by a faculty whose members each gave up five percent of their annual income (in the midst of the Great Depression) to cover Tillich's salary. Tillich hoped accordingly that the conditions in Germany would improve so that he could go back. This hope lasted until December of 1933 when he received a letter from the Nazi Ministry of Culture informing him that, because of his writings and political affiliation, he would be ineligible for employment should he return. The last door to the old world was now closed.

Remaining in America brought with it, then, the need to find secure employment—a difficult challenge given the economic conditions of the time. No less of an obstacle was the challenge of learning English. Toward the end of his life Tillich acknowledged this obstacle directly: "To begin life anew in the United States at forty-seven years of age and without even a minimum knowledge of the language was rather difficult" (*ET,* op. cit., p. 265). While students at Union initially found his pronunciation of various words humorous, they kindly assisted him, as did his colleagues, in speaking and writing. Eventually, though his thick accent never departed, Tillich was able to communicate his highly abstract ideas in a language much more concrete than his own to a culture much more practical than his own. The achievement has not been lost on his biographers. As Marion Pauck observes, "The mere fact that his complex and sometimes obscure thought was accepted in an intellectual climate marked by practicality is astonishing" ("Introduction to the Perennial Classics Edition" in *Dynamics of Faith* [hereafter, *DF*], HarperCollins, 2001, p. xiii).

What made Tillich's ideas so successful in spite of the language barrier? Why was he subsequently rehired and then promoted by Union, invited to be a distinguished university professor at Harvard after his retirement from the seminary in 1955, and finally pictured on the cover of TIME magazine as America's "foremost Protestant thinker" in 1959? On what basis did crowds across the country gather to hear him speak at churches and universities right up to his death in 1965? Answers vary. One consistent reason, however, seems to be that Tillich had a gift for "reading the times" in a way that spoke to people, always with an eye to how the Christian faith could provide a meaningful and relevant response to the general predicament in question—particularly to those for whom the conventional answers of Sunday School religiosity (i.e., "just believe") had lost their power.

The best example of Tillich's ability to read and respond to the times appears in his description of the "sacred void" that had opened following the Second World War. Moving away from his focus on politics (due, in part, to the advice of his colleague, Reinhold Niebuhr), Tillich began to explore what he characterized as a general malaise or sense of emptiness that had come to dominate parts of mid-twentieth century America and Europe. This development, he argued, was the result of a massive cultural transition occasioned by the unspeakable calamities of the previous decade as well as the emerging threat of atomic warfare. As Taylor explains, "The demonisms of German Nazism and of World War II had run their course and now Tillich saw humankind suspended in an inner void, a vacuum, laden with an angst that theologians of culture must address" (Taylor, op. cit., p. 119). To aid him in his description of the new situation, Tillich turned to two modes of thought popular at the time—depth psychology (which focuses on the role of the unconscious in waking life) and existentialism.

Existentialism, a modern philosophy that underscores the freedom human beings have to create their own identities through major life-decisions in a universe bereft of purpose, had for Tillich expressed the mood of the day precisely. While many of existentialism's Christian opponents either rejected it or, as is often the case today, simply scoffed at what they did not understand, Tillich viewed the philosophy sympathetically in spite of the fact that its most famous proponents were atheists. Part of the reason for his open attitude was his early encounter with Heidegger's thought while at Marburg. Yet even Tillich struggled. "It took years," he writes, "before I became fully aware of the impact of this encounter on my own thinking. I resisted, I tried to learn, I accepted the new ways of thinking even more than the answers it gave" (*ET,* op. cit., p. 262). Existentialism had appeal to the theologian because it diagnosed human life for what it is—a fleeting existence characterized by dread and despair concerning the inevitability of death, the awareness of which had become especially acute in the "spiritual void" that followed the war.

Tillich's dialogue with existentialism came to pervade his theology by the early 1950s. He believed it brought to the surface features of human existence most of us try to avoid, often to our own spiritual or psychological peril. For this reason he considered existentialism the "natural ally" of the Christian faith: once a theologian has examined and drawn upon the analysis of human existence existentialism provides, he can address it from a faith perspective. Tillich says the same thing about depth-psychology and Freudian psychoanalysis: "The interpretation of man's predicament by psychoanalysis raises the question that is implied in man's very existence. Systematic theology has to show that the religious symbols [of biblical faith] are answers to this question" (*Theology of Culture* [hereafter, *TC*], Oxford University Press, 1959, p. 125). By *question* Tillich refers here to that of meaning. What constitutes the ultimate significance of our lives, particularly when many of us no longer find the answers religion has traditionally provided to be compelling or persuasive? For a response, Tillich excavated the Jewish and Christian Scriptures for gems of insight that, with a little modern polish and some reinterpretation, might speak again to such a question. The method of correlation (his way of doing theology) had thus been born.

What Tillich called the method of correlation did not, as a matter of fact, originate with him. Other theologians as well as the authors of the New Testament had been adapting the Christian message instinctively to changing "predicaments" or circumstances since the faith began, an observation Tillich himself made toward the end of his theological career. All the same, Tillich gave a name to the method and refined it like nobody had before. So popular was his attempt to update the Christian faith by translating its ancient symbols and language into modern terms which brought spiritual-psychological *healing* (the original meaning of the word "salvation" in Latin) that he became known as the "therapeutic theologian." One young woman even claimed that reading his most famous work, *The Courage to Be* (1952), prevented her from committing suicide. There was, she found, a path to confronting the threat of meaninglessness in the modern era—and Tillich paved it.

Tillich's publication of *The Courage to Be* marked the first wave in a tide of literary activity that would last until 1963. During this period, which began with a publication of his sermons in 1948, he wrote dozens of articles and books, including his three-volume *Systematic Theology* (1951, 1957, 1963); a treatment of ethics and how they stem from the dynamics of being (*Love, Power and Justice*, 1954); a collection of essays on the religious impulse as the actual (though often hidden) force behind cultural expression (*Theology of Culture*, 1951); an effort to show the compatibility of biblical language with philosophical thinking (*Biblical Religion and the Search for Ultimate Reality*, 1955); and a look at other religions from an inclusive Christian perspective (*Christianity and the Encounter of the World Religions*, 1963). We will return to several of these texts along with the aforementioned *Dynamics of Faith* (1957), Tillich's primer on the meaning of faith, as well as *The Irrelevance and Relevance of the Christian Message* (1963), later in our discussion. For now one point suffices: by the end of this, the most prolific chapter of Tillich's adult career, his influence "in both the secular and religious communities was rivaled only by the writings of his colleague, Reinhold Niebuhr" (James Livingston, *Modern Christian Thought: from the Enlightenment to Vatican II*, Macmillan, 1971, p. 141). He had finally arrived.

Yet Tillich was also not without his critics. In 1963, now at the end of his most productive writing period and at the height of his popularity in America, the German immigrant turned America's premier Protestant thinker stood before an "overflow audience" in Berkeley, California, as Christian fundamental-ists and left-wing radicals alike picketed outside (Durwood Foster, "Introduction" in *The Irrelevance and Relevance of the Christian Message* [hereafter, *IRCM*], Pilgrim Press, 1996, p. ix). One group chided Tillich for his criticism of bibli-cal literalism, the other presumably for his association with religion. We also know, as Matthew Lon Weaver of the North American Paul Tillich Society reports, that "even if Tillich was not self-consciously political as he had formerly been [in Ger-many], J. Edgar Hoover's FBI believed his politics to be worthy of observation until his dying day" (*Bulletin of the North American Paul Tillich Society*, vol. 30, no. 2, 2004, p. 28). In particular they considered Tillich suspicious due to the support he provided to incoming émigrés from Europe up through the Second World War as well as his association with groups that were critical of McCarthyism throughout the following decade. The fact that he depicted "McCarthy's Influence as 'Potential Fascism'" in a speech covered by the *Harvard Crimson* in 1956 probably did not help (*Ibid*).

A group of critics more vocal than the FBI and much greater in number were the traditionalist Christians of his time. Today, echoes of their criticism appear across the internet where conservative-fundamentalist websites dismiss Tillich as a liberal and those who cite him as somehow unchristian. But even to men and women in Tillich's day who identified them-selves as conventional in their beliefs without being dogmatic, the theology he presented posed a threat. Why? The answer, as D. Mackenzie Brown observes in a dialogue with Tillich in 1963, is that for some he makes "paradoxical statements which weaken people's confidence in symbols and liturgies and churches. And [he tends] to destroy their belief, without giving them anything to replace it" (*Ultimate Concern: Tillich in Dialogue*, Harper & Row, 1970 [1965], p. 188). Brown then confronts Tillich directly. "Dr. Tillich," he asks, "Are you not a dangerous man?" Could it be, he adds, that "[w]hen you broadcast your concepts," including the idea (which we will subsequently discuss) that God does not *literally* exist, "you harm those people who are unable to comprehend" and lead them as a result to "misapply your ideas?"

In the dialogue Tillich responds immediately by agreeing with the label. Dangerous applies! Yet the risk is worth it: "There are thinking people who do not doubt, although I cannot imagine how this is possible; but there are also many thinking people who do doubt and even more of them who have doubted but do so no longer. They have simply rejected Christianity and every other religion. This is the actual situation. Now who speaks for them?" (*Ibid.*, p. 190). Here, toward the end of his life, we see Tillich's sense of mission unfold with brilliant clarity in spite of whatever the critics finally had to say. He had become in America "the apostle to the intellectuals." More generally, he spoke to any thinking person who questioned faith. That was his task, his calling, his charge, his life, and his legacy.

After the interview Tillich returned to the University of Chicago where he had the year prior (1962) been appointed to a faculty position created specifically for him. We can only imagine what it must have been like: one of the most tumultuous decades of American history was now underway. The Civil Rights movement had begun. A president had been shot. A theology proclaiming "the death of God" was gaining momentum. And there he was, a career at three American institutions of higher learning now almost behind him, a "dangerous man" protested and picketed, yet also an individual who had managed to reach through sermons, books, articles, and lectures many people who craved *something more* for their lives, something beyond the constant cycle of wanting and acquiring material goods or success, but could not find it in the language of conventional Christianity or fundamentalist faith. Indeed, as Brown had noted in dialogue with Tillich, he had become "the most influential theologian of the twentieth century" (*Ibid.*, p.

188) and all of this on the eve of America's greatest cultural revolution.

But the theologian who survived Verdun and Nazism, the one who braved the American new world and confronted all the uncertainties that came with immigration and starting life again at 47, would never see it. On October 22, 1965, Tillich died of a heart attack. To a younger American chaplain and one of his last students, he shared the following words shortly before he passed away: "Ya, chaplain, there was a time when I thought I could do almost anything by sheer will power, but now I am beginning to learn that I am really finite, not just theoretically finite" (Donald Arthur, "Paul Tillich as a Military Chaplain," unpublished essay, 1999, p. 17). Shortly thereafter in a hospital room tucked away from the noise of a world he was just about to leave behind forever, he confided to his wife, "Today is dying day" (Pauck, op. cit., p. 283). Life for our theologian had come to its end, but his enormous literary output—particularly from 1948 to 1963—had shaken the ground of twentieth century despair and meaninglessness, calling the saints of modernity to emerge from their spiritual tombs.

CHAPTER THREE

MEANING

The problem of meaninglessness, as we discussed last chapter, was one that Tillich argued had become more visible by the middle of the twentieth century due (in part) to the calamities and devastation of the Second World War. Americans and Europeans found themselves in a spiritual void. Anguish over the perceived emptiness of life was now the psycho-spiritual predicament of many people. Coming to such a realization and diagnosing the collective condition was the theologian of culture's basic task. Once the theologian of culture knew the condition, Tillich reasoned, he could interpret the Christian message in ways that would actually meet the needs or predicament of those who heard it. Of course, no prescription could guarantee successful results; whatever cure there might be would happen *to* people, perhaps through the words of another, but they could not produce it themselves. Tillich accordingly hoped for the appearance of redemptive or "sacred possibilities" that would heal and empower people to overcome (however fragmentarily) the split between themselves and their divine "ground" or source of wholeness—God.

The most extensive diagnosis of the modern spiritual predicament from Tillich's perspective appears in *The Courage to Be*. There he attributes the source of what he calls existential anxiety (i.e., non-pathological anxiety) to the precarious nature of human existence in general. Some degree of anxiety, he says, is *natural* to the human condition. We are finite creatures, estranged from our true or essential being and its foundation in being-itself or God (we will discuss what Tillich means by being-itself in chapters six and seven). While we continue to share in and derive our "power of being" from the radiating depth of being-itself, we face threats to the full affirmation of our actual being on a variety of levels—physical, psychological and spiritual. These threats cause anxiety. Any of them can diminish or even eradicate our individual or "ontic" being. To confront these threats in a life-affirming way we must understand the various forms of anxiety within us to which such threats give rise. Only then, Tillich suggests, can the Christian message and its symbols be interpreted in a way that might speak to the problem.

What, then, are the various forms of existential anxiety? We already know one: the anxiety over meaning and its loss in the modern age. In centuries past other forms of anxiety dominated Western culture. Consider the final chapter of the Middle Ages. At that time, Tillich argues, the concern was not whether human existence had meaning, but whether self-perceived sinners were acceptable to God. Tillich labels this dread of damnation the anxiety of condemnation and guilt. He writes, "The anxiety of condemnation symbolized as the 'wrath of God' and intensified by the imagery of hell and purgatory drove people of the late Middle Ages to try various means of assuaging their anxiety" (*CTB*, op. cit., pp. 58-59). These ways included the purchase of indulgences to obtain God's forgiveness, long pilgrimages to holy sites, and the observation of holy relics, all of which were prompted by the anguishing question of how one could appease an ostensibly wrathful and angry God. The Protestant Reformation confronted condemnation-anxiety, in turn, by empowering and reassuring its victims that God through Christ loved them *without any merit on their part*. Justification by *grace* was (re)born.

By the time we get to the twentieth century, of course, things had changed. Modern people, Tillich observes, typically no longer find themselves in the grip of condemnation-anxiety. They wrestle instead with the problem of meaning and the threat of its loss. They live in a "disenchanted" universe, as the philosopher and political economist Max Weber labeled it, thanks to what Tillich calls the emergence of technical-scientific knowledge that, beginning in the seventeenth century, sacrificed a sense of nature's spiritual depth for the sake of manipulating and controlling it. They feel alone in an indifferent world, yet they press forward—blindly, desperately—never looking down for fear of seeing a bottomless abyss beneath their feet. They search. Some eventually give themselves over to despair or cynicism and their lives break down. Others cling to the conventional form of a religious faith only to grow weary and fall away. Whatever path they take the predicament remains the same: "Everything is tried and nothing satisfies. The contents of the [religious] tradition, however excellent, however praised, however loved once, lose their power to give content *today*" (*Ibid.*, p. 48; italics original).

The experience of meaninglessness as Tillich understands it points to the encounter that human beings can have with nonbeing: "Emptiness and loss of meaning are expressions of the threat of nonbeing to the spiritual life" (*Ibid*). Nonbeing marks Tillich's way of discussing that which threatens or diminishes the fullness of our being or the actualization of our potential. The courage to be is that power within us that resists the threat of nonbeing. It is the power of being (i.e., God) working through us that enables us to affirm life, the courage—as Tillich puts it—"to say yes to one's own life and life in general, in spite of the driving forces of fate, in spite of the insecurities of daily existence, in spite of the catastrophes of existence and the breakdown of meaning" (*The New Being* [hereafter, *NB*], Charles Scribner's Sons, 1955, p. 53). This is invariably the character of such courage: it works in spite of threats to our complete self-actualization like meaninglessness or life-denying guilt, for the glory of God is not a man reduced to ashes but—as the second century theologian Ireneaus once put it—"man fully alive."

Here, however, we meet a challenging problem. If God "desires" for us fullness of being, a flourishing that goes beyond mere survival, or what Jesus in John's Gospel calls "abundant life" (10:10), and if God is that power in us enabling us to resist nonbeing, what comprises the source of nonbeing itself? From where does this life-destroying force originate? The short answer is this: because we are estranged from God and "stand out" from being-itself, we are susceptible to the disintegrating power of nonbeing in a way that the source of being (i.e., being-itself or God) is not. Such disintegration can affect us physically (as in death) as well as spiritually (as in the loss of meaning which results in "existential despair"). The good news is that we receive the power from being-itself to resist nonbeing in these forms. Even in the most crippling moments of existential despair, therefore, the power of being—the power to say "yes" once again to life—remains active and potentially victorious so long as one continues to have being.

The precursor of existential despair according to Tillich is doubt. This does not mean that doubt and the courage to be (or what Tillich sometimes calls "absolute faith") are inherently antithetical. Doubt naturally exists as part of faith because we are separated from that to which we essentially belong. If God and human beings enjoyed complete union doubt would not be possible, but that is not the way things are. "Man," Tillich explains, "is able to ask because he is separated from, while participating in, what he is asking about. In every question an element of doubt, the awareness of not having, is implied" (CTB, op. cit., p. 48). The gap between God and humanity, in other words, not only makes doubt possible but also constitutes "a condition of all spiritual life" (Ibid). A problem occurs only when doubt as an element of faith (which is normal) becomes total, comprehensive, and all-consuming. The result is a feeling of emptiness, loss, and despair, all of which point to a sense of complete separation from that which formerly gave one meaning.

Tillich addresses the prevalence of existential despair among his contemporaries in a 1957 essay for *The Saturday Evening Post*. To show how religion can address the problem he begins by clarifying what "religion" means. Many people, he says, often assume religion concerns the belief in the existence of God or a set of rituals and activities one performs in relation to a deity. Yet a closer examination yields a different meaning. As the scholar James Livingston explains, religion from Tillich's perspective refers to "the *depth dimension* in all of our cultural and spiritual life. What Tillich means by the use of the metaphor 'depth' is that the religious dimension of life points to what is ultimate and unconditional in life; i.e., what sustains one's being and gives meaning to one's life" (Livingston, op. cit., p. 141, italics original). The trouble is that people have lost access to this deeper dimension of their being. Modern daily life, says Tillich, incessantly "runs ahead; every moment is filled with something that must be done or seen or said or planned" (*ET*, op. cit., p. 3). This way of being prevents individuals from taking a moment to consider the deeper meaning of their lives. Instinctively they ignore its loss by distracting themselves in a flurry of activity that always presses forward without ultimately considering where it is going or why.

Here we must pause: How does Tillich know that anxiety over the loss of meaning truly constitutes a problem for modern people? From where does he derive such a judgment? The problem, he says, becomes evident through an analysis of culture. Tillich identifies art, literature, and philosophy (especially in the form of existentialism) as the primary vehicles of cultural expression. These avenues of creativity are the "places," Tillich writes, "where the awareness of the predicament of Western man in our period is most sharply expressed. . . . It is both the subject matter and style of these creations that show the passionate and often tragic struggle about the meaning of life in a period in which man has lost the dimension of depth" (*Ibid.,* p. 5). One example Tillich seems to have in mind is Pablo Picasso's "Guernica" (1937), a painting that distorts and reconfigures a variety of human and animal forms, all of which appear to be in anguish. Tillich interprets work of this kind religiously: "It is the religious question that is asked when the painter breaks the visible surface into pieces, then reunites them into a great picture that has little similarity with the world at which we normally look, but that expresses our anxiety and our courage to face reality" (*Ibid.*, p. 6). Unfortunately, while the artist may implicitly raise the question of meaning and its loss, those responsible in the religious or self-help sector for supplying responses that speak to the problem often fail.

How, then, does one face the problem directly? Where can a person turn if he wishes to do more than simply adjust to the fast pace of meaningless contemporary life? Is there a way to confront the emptiness of merely going forward, of acquiring more and more without any destination, purpose, or aim? There is, says Tillich. To find it, he advises his reader first to interrupt his daily routine and raise the question of meaning, for "[o]nly if he has moments in which he does not care about what comes next can he experience the meaning of this moment here and now and ask himself about the meaning of his life" (*Ibid.*, p. 3). One can imagine here the kind of resistance Tillich received from those who instinctively knew the danger of pausing to consider the true meaning of their existence. "We dare not stop," as the former Harvard chaplain Peter Gomes more recently observes, "lest in the stillness we are overwhelmed by the sound of our own anxieties and fears" ("Introduction to the Second Edition" in *CTB*, op. cit., p. xvii).

Yet what would happen if a person could stop, however briefly? Might the sense of what Tillich calls his "ultimate concern" (which we will discuss in the next chapter) bubble up from the deepest recesses of his being? Would he be able to hear those concerns, as Livingston puts it, "that undergird and give meaning to [his] existence" (Livingston, op. cit., p. 141), concerns that take him beyond immediate interests and necessities to those that direct the orientation of his whole being to something greater than himself? Could he unplug himself from a consumerism that thrives on the creation and gratification of surface desires, so much so that it promotes the mockery of deep questions that might unchain him from its bondage? If he could, Tillich says, he may begin to feel or at least prepare himself to rediscover what is truly important to him, inviting the presence of meaning back into his life. This does not imply that the clouds of despair would suddenly part, nor does it signify that he could resolve the loss of meaning simply by being still, but it does suggest that he who stops to face the absence of meaning in his life might be a step closer at least to its partial recovery. The question, of course, is how.

The way to regain the dimension of depth begins with the admission that it has been lost. "Such awareness," Tillich explains, "is in itself a state of being grasped by that which is symbolized in the term, dimension of depth. He who realizes that he is separated from the ultimate source of meaning shows by his realization that he is separated but is also reunited" (*ET*, op. cit., p. 7). Disillusion may lessen its grip when the question of meaning overtakes the individual and inspires him to seek that which he feels is now missing. In the process, while he may be unable to possess a conceptual answer to the question of his life's meaning, he can be grasped by the power of the question itself which awakens and reorients him to what he has lost. Being grasped by the question of meaning accordingly marks a crucial step in the direction of recovering the lost dimension of depth by rekindling a desire for that from which one feels separated. The meaningfulness of our lives ultimately finds expression in our *posture* toward the source of meaning, the depth of our lives and existence—not in its *possession*.

A hundred years before Tillich another Lutheran thinker advocated the same kind of posture toward the source of meaning. He called the posture "faith" and he identified the source of meaning as "God." True faith, he said, consists not in what we think we know about God but in how we *relate* to God. Indeed, he told his readers, a pagan who worships an idol in a foreign land but does so passionately and with his whole being can be *in the truth* more than a Christian who worships the "true" God but in a lukewarm or indifferent way. The thinker in question was Kierkegaard, and the advice he gave for recovering the faith that had been lost in his time because of indifference nicely anticipates what Tillich would suggest a century later: "Let him despair of ever becoming a Christian himself," Kierkegaard writes, "even so, he may be closer than he thinks" (*Concluding Unscientific Postscript to Philosophical Fragments*, ed. Howard and Edna Hong, vol. 1, Princeton University Press, 1992, p. 229). To address the most common form of modern anxiety, that of meaninglessness, a person must likewise acknowledge the loss of meaning in his life. Such a confession, to use more traditional religious vocabulary, paradoxically reestablishes a relationship with that from which the one has been estranged, potentially supplying the power once again to affirm oneself in spite of the threat to the spiritual dimension of one's being that meaninglessness poses.

There are, of course, other thinkers besides Kierkegaard upon whom Tillich relies or to whom Tillich responds when it comes to his view of the courage to be, the existential anxieties that plague humankind, and the methods one can use to help people reconnect with that from which they have been separated. Much of Tillich's stress on the courage to be as the affirmation of life that lies at the heart of the Christian faith, for instance, owes a major debt to the philosopher Friedrich Nietzsche who criticized Christianity as a life-denying religion. Tillich agrees that *genuine* Christianity should enhance human life, not buckle it. When someone like Nietzsche offers such criticism Tillich shows his readers why Christians ought to be open to its truth, particularly insofar as it might help them reclaim what has been buried by neglect or distortion. Indeed, when Nietzsche derides the disciples of Jesus as they appear in the Gospels for appearing heavy, glum, joyless, and burdened in spite of being "redeemed," Tillich pauses to consider the criticism seriously: "We should subject ourselves to the piercing force of these words, and should ask ourselves, 'Is our lack of joy due to the fact that we are Christians, or to the fact that we are not sufficiently Christian?' Perhaps we . . . can show that this is a distortion of the truth" (*NB*, op. cit., p. 141).

Tillich's willingness to consider criticism of the Christian religion provides a rare example of how a person of faith might benefit from listening to those perspectives with which he would ordinarily disagree. One can also see why many regarded Tillich's openness to such criticism as a threat, especially insofar as he recognized the (partial) validity of atheism, including Nietzsche's version (of which Tillich was also critical). We will come back to Tillich's stance on atheism when we discuss his understanding of God. We will also consider later in our discussion how Jesus the Christ ultimately conquers the problem of meaninglessness according to Tillich beyond what we have covered here.

For now the reader should have a preliminary grasp of Tillich's response to the threat of meaninglessness: by identifying and then naming the problem thanks to a thorough analysis of contemporaneous cultural forms, Tillich hoped to provide people with an authentic way of recovering what they had lost. This attempt to get his audience to pause and acknowledge the loss of meaning they were experiencing rested on the conviction that, in so doing, they could be "grasped" again by the question of meaning itself and discover buried beneath the immediate desires or distractions of everyday activities what ultimately mattered to them. Only then, Tillich insisted, could people seriously confront the problem of meaninglessness and perhaps break through to a new and deeper sense of meaning in their lives.

Tillich's reference to what concerns or matters to a person ultimately and his use "ultimate concern" in the place of "faith" marks his attempt to translate the latter term into language that would not alienate people who found themselves on the periphery of the Christian religion. The term faith, he maintains, is prone to misunderstanding. Often it prompts people to think that they must sacrifice their minds by believing in something absurd that contradicts modern science. What, then, does faith understood as ultimate concern mean for Tillich, and what views of faith does he reject? To answer these questions we turn now from the problem of meaning and its loss to Tillich's view of the nature of faith which he discusses at length in his classic book, *The Dynamics of Faith*. There we will see not only how he reinterprets the meaning of the word faith, but also how he does so in a way that overcomes the antithesis between science and religion in order to make God a possibility again for people of the modern world.

CHAPTER FOUR

FAITH

Many people, religious or otherwise, assume that doubt and faith are antithetical. If a person at a Bible study raises questions about the historical verifiability of a narrative in Scripture, for example, she may receive criticism from others in the group for her apparent lack of faith. The reason for this kind of reaction, as the Tillich scholars Donald Musser and Joseph Price explain, is that people often confuse faith with belief: "In popular religious usage, the term faith suggests the pattern of believing in an assertion that somehow ignores reason or requires acceptance without empirical or logical evidence" (*Tillich,* Abingdon Press, 2010, p. 51). When people maintain that faith amounts to nothing more than believing something without evidence, in other words, then faith and doubt are indeed contrary. But if faith constitutes an *attitude of trust* in something larger than oneself, something upon which a person risks the ultimate fulfillment of her being, yet something from which she remains separated, then faith necessarily involves doubt. "If doubt appears," therefore, "it should not be considered as the negation of faith, but as an element which was always and will always be present in the act of faith" (*DF,* op. cit., p. 25). Such doubt actually confirms faith: "It indicates the seriousness of the concern, its unconditional character" (*Ibid*).

To some the argument that doubt exists in any faith commitment may not sound that extraordinary, but consider the implication: those who boast of being "true believers" because they repress questions about their faith or refuse to allow others the opportunity to raise such questions may possess the weakest faith of all. Indeed, as Tillich's contemporary H. Richard Niebuhr observes, "A faith in God so unsure of itself or rather of God that it does not permit men to listen to criticism is a very shaky thing indeed" ("Foreword" in Ludwig Feuerbach, *The Essence of Christianity*, trans. George Eliot, Harper & Row, 1957, p. viii). Obviously this does not mean that ministers and other church leaders should force people to question their faith, but neither (Tillich argues) should they discourage those who openly and honestly express their doubts. Sincere doubt, the type that genuinely seeks answers to the questions it asks, gives faith a vital and dynamic character, the kind that Jacob symbolizes in wrestling with the angelic presence of God (Genesis 32:24-30) and that Jesus epitomizes when he asks one of the most haunting questions in Scripture, his last: "My God, my God, why have you forsaken me?" (Mark 15:34).

Whatever we might think today, the claim that faith includes an element of doubt made Tillich enormously popular after the publication of his *Dynamics of Faith* in 1957, particularly among mainline Protestant college students who were probably relieved to hear that questioning the faith of their religious upbringing was not a sin. This concise book, merely six chapters and under 150 pages in length, marked Tillich's way of introducing his theology to an entire generation of young people. It became an invitation to consider a whole new way of thinking—not only about faith, but also about its relationship to courage, the nature and limits of religious language, the "existence" of God, the significance of Jesus understood as the Christ, the rise of criticism regarding the truth of the Bible, and even the question of truth (and its connection to faith) itself. The heavy and daunting nature of these topics, however, suggests a challenge evident to anyone (including the present author) who has taught Tillich's theology in a church setting or college classroom: Tillich's introduction requires an introduction! His thought is dense. It needs unpacking.

This chapter proceeds, then, by exploring first what Tillich sees as the most common misconceptions of faith. Once they are clear, we will examine Tillich's presentation of faith itself as a person's "ultimate concern," that is, her reason for being or whatever she values most in her life. As the reader may guess, Tillich's view of faith as synonymous with being ultimately concerned about something will allow him to argue that faith does not belong solely to the Christian, the Muslim, or the Jew; it is a universal human phenomenon. All people have faith insofar as they have some object of ultimate concern in their lives that gives or promises them a sense of purpose, meaning, fulfillment or security. The question is whether the object of one's ultimate concern (i.e., one's god or God) is truly ultimate. Many gods—including those of nation and race that Tillich encountered under the shadow of Nazism as well as those of success or social status that Tillich confronted in America—cannot fulfill what they promise. They are finite, and our *absolute* or unconditional trust in them inevitably leads in the end to disillusionment and despair. Lesser gods (or idols) always let us down.

The reason Tillich reinterprets faith the way he does will occupy us at the end of the chapter. Remember that Tillich was highly conscious of the fact that his audience consisted primarily of people who were "modern in culture and secular in sensibility" (Kelsey, op. cit., p. 87). His goal, then, was to show them how a proper understanding of faith, one that clears aside the ways in which popular opinion distorts its true meaning, could resolve the unnecessary conflict between religion and science. Both religion and science are legitimate, he argues, but they each speak to a different dimension or facet of existence. They are two swords that should never cross, as the historian of religion Martin Marty would say. Science as a methodology (i.e., a way of obtaining empirical knowledge) restricts itself by definition to the arena of objects in space and time and how they relate to one another. Whenever a scientist affirms or denies "God," therefore, she does no longer as a scientist since God, who "grounds" space and time without being an object *in* space and time, resides outside the scope of her inquiry. Religion, on the other hand, expresses that which human beings experience as the dimension of ultimacy in their lives. Faith, in turn, simply refers to being "grasped" by this dimension. It is a *state*, as the theologian John Haught puts it, "of allowing oneself to be drawn into the timeless and endless depth of being, meaning, goodness, truth and beauty that theists call God" (*God and the New Atheism*, Westminster John Knox Press, 2008, p. 54). Modern people can, in short, be religious and accept science; these approaches to reality point to different but non-contradictory dimensions of existence.

If faith refers to a state of being "grasped" by whatever matters most in a person's life, why do people so often wrongly equate it with belief? One answer is historical-cultural: since the seventeenth century and the rise of science, Americans and Western Europeans have largely come to see truth in "referential" terms: something is true only if it *refers* to an event that actually happened or an object that exists in the world. This, however, is only one kind of truth (and, taken by itself, a reductive and impoverished one). As the biblical scholars Christian Hauer and William Young explain, "Statements that are referentially 'false' or at least 'unverifiable' may be true in other respects" (*An Introduction to the Bible*, Prentice Hall, 2001, p. 30).

In the case of Christianity, Tillich says, the restriction of truth to the question of empirical verifiability surfaces when its proponents take its symbols, which point to the *ultimate* origin of human life or our separation from it (as the fall of Adam and his expulsion from the garden represents in Genesis 3), and interpret them as events that did or did not happen once upon a time in the not-so-distant past (*ET*, op. cit., p. 4). The test of faith, in turn, becomes whether one can—with little or no evidence—*believe* that these things refer to events that actually happened. Either the person convinces herself they did, often at great expense to the integrity of her mind, or she does not, in which case she finds herself on the periphery of her faith or beyond it altogether. But this is not the way it has to be. Reducing faith to a belief or "act of knowledge that has a low degree of evidence" (*DF*, op. cit., p. 36) reflects a common distortion of faith, one that has exercised "a tremendous power over popular thinking and [has] been largely responsible for alienating many from religion since the beginning of the scientific age" (*Ibid.*, p. 35). Genuine faith is something different.

Altogether, then, Tillich identifies three ways people distort the true meaning of faith, each of which he associates with a specific function of the human personality: cognition (the head), emotion (the heart), and volition (the will). These functions filter the great light of faith or ultimate concern as it projects itself outward from the core of the self onto that screen which, when given symbolic expression, becomes the focal point or object of a person's faith (i.e., one's god or God). Head, heart, and will give faith its color and definition, but they do not make up the light of faith itself. They presuppose it. If we identify any of these functions as the source of faith we distort it, reducing it to something which it is not.

Examples of faith in its distorted forms are easy to find. If someone assumes she is a Christian because she rejects evolution by affirming the biblical account of creation as a referential truth, she obviously believes something, but belief of this kind is merely cognitive. It does not involve her whole heart and soul (Deuteronomy 6:5). Tillich writes: "The Christian may believe the Biblical writers, but not unconditionally. He does not have faith in them. He should not even have faith in the Bible. Faith is more than trust in even the most sacred authority. It is participation in the subject of one's ultimate concern with one's whole being" (*Ibid.*, p. 38). As a counter-example to our creationist, think of the Apostle Paul. Do Christians see him as a man of faith because he was "Bible-believing" or because God through Jesus Christ was his reason for being, his ultimate concern? The answer should be obvious. Faith does not amount merely to believing something, even if it requires what Tillich calls "concrete content" for its actualization. It grasps the whole person.

Faith, likewise, does not (for Tillich) amount simply to a matter of the heart or an act of will. Since faith grasps the entire person, it does not belong exclusively to the sphere of one's private feelings even though feeling obviously plays a role in its expression. The same is true of volition. When a person thinks of her faith in terms of "deciding for Christ," for example, she reduces faith to a once-and-for-all act of will instead of seeing it as being claimed by an ultimate concern *prior* to the verbal articulation of her commitment. While her will contributes to the actualization of her ultimate concern, the concern itself comes first. This we know even in the case of love: a bride may profess her commitment to a groom, but the profession she makes presupposes the fact that she is already grasped by her partner's love. Her vow does not bring her love into being. So too in matters of faith: "No command to believe and no will to believe can create faith" (*Ibid.*, p. 44). We cannot force ourselves to will something or believe something arbitrarily just because a preacher or "the Bible" demands it. We must, says Tillich, be grasped at the core of our being by something larger than ourselves.

Readers who recall earlier references to the influence of the Lutheran tradition on Tillich's perspective may recognize its influence here as well. Luther, following St. Augustine's interpretation of the Apostle Paul, argues that faith (which Luther, like Tillich, defines in terms of trust rather than mere belief) is never a "work" (i.e., a deed one must perform to earn God's love) of human beings; if it were, we could never be sure if the amount of faith we have would measure up to God's standards. Instead, as the Apostle Paul writes, God "measures out" the gift of faith to us (Romans 12:3) which becomes, in turn, the means by which we receive salvation—the healing power of God that makes us whole again. "Faith means being grasped by a power greater than we are," Tillich explains in more contemporary terms, "a power that shakes us and turns us, and transforms us and heals us" (*NB*, op. cit., p. 38). Notice the emphasis. Only God can turn us to God. Faith is not something we do of our own volition; it is something we *find ourselves doing.*

In classical Lutheran teaching the emphasis upon God as the source and author of salvation, as the one who reconciles humanity to Godself (2 Corinthians 5:19), finds its sharpest expression in the statement that human beings are "justified by grace through faith" (Ephesians 2:8). Tillich explains the meaning of this phrase carefully to students at the Divinity School of the University of Chicago toward the end of his career:

> The justifying power [i.e., that which makes a person acceptable to God as evident in the phrase, justification by grace through faith] is the divine grace; the channel through which men receive this grace is faith. Faith is by no means the cause, but only the channel. In the moment in which faith is understood as the cause of justification, it is a worse work of man than anything in Roman Catholicism. It results in destroying one's own honesty by compelling oneself to believe certain things. This is the consequence of the phrase, justification *by* faith. If faith is a human work which makes us acceptable to God, and if this work is the cause or basis of our salvation, then we can never be certain of our salvation in the sense in which Luther sought for certainty when he asked the question, 'How do I find a merciful God?' Therefore, whenever you are dealing with Protestant theology, dismiss forever this distortion of faith—*sola fide* in Latin—which sees faith as a cause instead of a channel. Luther made this clear repeatedly when he said that faith is always receiving and only receiving; it does not produce anything (*A History of Christian Thought*, ed. Carl Braaten, Simon and Schuster, 1968, pp. 308-309, italics original).

Faith does not make a person acceptable to God. God is the one who heals and accepts us. Grace saves; faith simply receives.

The meaning of faith according to Tillich should thus be clear: it involves the whole person and cannot be reduced to an act of will, a belief we hold, or what our hearts tell us. Instead, faith unites heart, mind, and will together in a total act of the personality, one which presupposes being grasped by a power greater than oneself. Indeed, faith makes the human personality possible insofar as it integrates its various functions, orienting them to the object of its concern. The corollary of Tillich's understanding of faith is that all people have faith—something they take with absolute seriousness in their lives. Even the atheist has faith. Her desire for truth and her absolute trust in science to get her there reflect an *a priori* or pre-rational confidence in something she cannot prove. She must, moreover, have faith in her own ability to make sense of what she observes. The same is true, say, of a research scientist trying to find a cure for cancer. She cannot prove a cure exists, but the desire to find it grasps her, causing her perhaps to make sacrifices in her personal life or forego other, less demanding types of employment for the sake of the promise that, once found, the cure she seeks will provide her with fulfillment.

Of course, people (including the atheist or the research scientist) are not always conscious of the faith that drives them, but faith remains present regardless. The heart, as St. Augustine observes, is restless. "Like all other creatures," says Livingston of Tillich's view, "human beings are concerned with those things that condition existence, such as food and shelter. But humans also have spiritual concerns that are urgent and claim ultimacy" (Livingston, op. cit., p. 141). These concerns presuppose what Tillich identifies as "an awareness of the infinite" to which we belong, which is to say that because human consciousness has the ability to rise above the immediacy of the present moment people have a sense of the greater totality of all things, a sense of what the theologian Friedrich Schleiermacher (who was a significant influence on Tillich) calls "the whole" or "the all." Nevertheless, human beings remain separate—like all other finite creatures—from the infinite totality of which they are uniquely aware. The heart, yearning to rest in the infinite (God), can give itself over to creative as well as destructive spiritual concerns. At worst it can substitute things of this world for the infinite even though only the latter (the argument goes) can provide lasting fulfillment.

In search of fulfillment and security human beings can make just about any finite reality into a god. Common examples include success, money, militaristic power, social status, a social cause, unrequited love, or even a nation. Not all of these realities are inherently bad. The desire for success, to cite one example, constitutes something natural insofar as human beings rightly seek vitality for themselves. But when the desire becomes all-consuming or causes a person to bring harm to herself or others for the sake of security promised by the god to whom she grants allegiance, the god in question has proven itself to be a demon. It "turn[s] on us and dominate[s] our lives," as the Jesuit theologian Dean Brackley explains (*The Call to Discernment in Troubled Times*, Crossroad, 2004, p. 14). The demonic refers accordingly in Tillich's theology to the destructive power which results from idolatrous faith. For someone grasped by this power, there is only bondage. If her god is a failure, the meaning of her life will crumble. Any threat must be resisted—desperately, sometimes violently.

The risk of faith, then, amounts to whether the god an individual worships is worth it. "Faith," Tillich writes, "risks the vanishing of the concrete god in whom it believes" (*DF*, op cit., pp. 20-21). Doubt can be a crucial ally in the resistance against idolatrous faith by helping a person distinguish what matters greatly in life (i.e., the country in which a person lives, the work a person does) from what matters—or should matter—most. Making anything finite into a god not only anticipates the likely breakdown of meaning in a person's life; it can also lead, as noted, to destruction and the suffering of others. Many Americans, for example, profess allegiance to "one nation, *under* God," but when its citizens believe their country is beyond criticism and can do no wrong, the nation (Tillich would say) takes the place of God. There is a big difference, in other words, between self-critical patriotism and nationalism. The latter constitutes idolatry, and the arrogance that comes with idolatry often leads to destruction (see Proverbs 16:18).

Tillich's view of doubt as an antidote to idolatry reflects his indebtedness once again to the Lutheran tradition as evident in Luther's critique of the late medieval Catholic Church and what Luther perceived to be its identification with God. The task of the Church, Luther maintains, is to point to God, not to substitute itself for God. This observation provides an instance of what Tillich calls "creative faith" or the Protestant Principle: "Only creative faith can resist the onslaught of destructive faith. Only the concern with what is truly ultimate can stand against idolatrous concerns" (*Ibid.,* p. 30). Nevertheless, doubt in service to such faith was something that was, for Tillich, at first hard to accept. Yet thanks to one of his early professors, the theologian Martin Kähler, Tillich was able to rethink his view of doubt. In an autobiographical reflection Tillich writes:

> The step I made in these years was the insight that the principle of justification through faith refers not only to the religious-ethical but also to the religious-intellectual life. Not only he who is in sin but also he who is in doubt is justified [i.e., accepted by God] through faith. The situation of doubt, even doubt about God, need not separate us from God. There is faith in every serious doubt, namely the faith in the truth as such, even if the only truth we can express is our lack of truth. But if this is experienced in its depth as an ultimate concern, the divine is present; and he who doubts in such an attitude is "justified" in his thinking (*The Protestant Era*, The University of Chicago Press, 1957, p. xiv).

Since we are unable to please God due to our estrangement from God, God accepts us by way of grace through faith.

This includes us in our doubt. The discovery, as Wilhelm and Marion Pauck tell us, brought Tillich immense relief (Pauck, op. cit., p. 19).

Tillich's subsequent affirmation of doubt not only as essential to the critique of idolatrous faith but also as an inherent element of faith due to our separation from God likewise brought immense relief to others, particularly those who found themselves uncertain as to whether their questioning was somehow inimical to faith. Now grace could resurface. God was big enough for their questions. Yet questions regarding *Tillich's* view of faith continue to linger. By defining faith as a total act of the personality whereby the entire individual is grasped by "something more," critics wonder, does Tillich violate free will? After all, does not the idea that faith amounts to being passively claimed by a greater power constitute an affront to the sense of self-agency and autonomy that modern people typically assume? Even when Tillich insists, as he does in one of his sermons, that one must "simply accept the fact that he is accepted [by God]," is it not the case that people—at least if they think of themselves as religious—must do *something* to obtain God's favor or mercy?

Let us for the sake of brevity reduce Tillich's likely response to two points. Note first that once one has been grasped by a power greater than oneself, our theologian describes faith as a "free and centered act" (*DF*, op. cit., p. 6). While a person cannot force herself to have faith, whatever power or powers claim her do not force her to surrender indefinitely. She can, recognizing perhaps the idolatrous nature of her god, cease and desist—however difficult or painful that may be. That said, she cannot by an act of will simply bring faith into being. She might entreat God for religious faith, if that is something she desires, but her "oscillating will" can neither produce nor sustain such faith on its own. Faith is a power that grasps a person, not something a person grasps by an act of the will. Once a person has been grasped, however, faith depends for its expression on the free act of the individual who takes the risk of affirming what matters most to her upon herself; in the process she can abandon or challenge her faith freely.

Note secondly that Tillich was not a determinist. He denies that "everything happens for a reason" or that God causes things to occur according to some kind of foreordained, mysterious plan. Human beings have freedom in making everyday choices, even if the infinite (understandably) must grasp them since it remains beyond their grasp. Tillich writes, "With respect to our fate and vocation we are free; with respect to our relation to God we are powerless" (*The Shaking of the Foundations* [hereafter, *SF*], Charles Scribner's Sons, 1948, p. 91). People have control over things "beneath them," as Luther puts it. God does not micromanage or interfere with human decisions or actions because God is not a being or person "out there," a tyrannical subject who makes us into "His" objects (*CTB*, op. cit., p. 185). Concerning matters *beyond* us, however, the wings of human willpower flutter in vain. "Only God," Tillich contends, "can reunite the estranged with himself" (*DF*, op. cit., p. 134). Only God can grasp and claim human beings.

Tillich's view of faith, his description of God, and his understanding of the affirmative role doubt can play in matters of ultimate concern all reveal the basic thrust of his theology: to discuss and answer "questions coming from the scientific and philosophical criticism of Christianity" (*PTTB*, op. cit., p. 321). Science and faith for this theologian point to different dimensions of existence: the former, to the realm of being in space and time; the latter, to the sacred depth and timeless ground of being from which all things derive their being. A rift between science and faith occurs only when people think of the ultimate in referential terms and objectify it as a god or a being "out there" that periodically intervenes in the course of history. Mere belief in this god falls short of genuine faith. As Tillich reminds us, "Faith is the state of being grasped by something that has *ultimate* meaning, and acting and thinking on the basis of this as a centered person" (*IRCM*, op. cit., p. 15; italics mine). It involves the whole person—mind, feelings, and will.

Much more could be said and asked about Tillich's view of faith. Does the fact, for example, that human beings have spiritual or ultimate concerns necessitate the "existence" of an ultimate dimension that corresponds to these concerns? Could it be, as the Jesuit theologian William O'Malley wonders, that we simply have a spiritual hunger for which there is no food? And what about those who do not feel they have been grasped by an ultimate concern? How would Tillich account for them? While further exploration of these questions and others like them extends beyond the scope of the present work, one question invites immediate attention: How, granting Tillich's view of the sacred, do we access this dimension of our existence beyond our concern for it? Seeking an answer, we consider next Tillich's analysis of religious symbols to show in what ways they can either facilitate or block access to God, the ultimate dimension and sacred depth of all being.

CHAPTER FIVE

SYMBOLS

An analysis of faith from Tillich's perspective has shown that it is not the sole property of theists (i.e., people who believe in a personal God), but a universal human phenomenon, one that integrates the personality by focusing it on a "reason for being" or an ultimate concern. Faith in this, its deeper sense, makes human personality possible by fusing together its functions (cognitive, volitional, and emotive) in a free and centered act of concern for that which matters most in a person's life. To the extent that one experiences the "unconditional demand" and promise of the concern, faith has the character of certainty. The individual finds himself undeniably in its grasp. As an example imagine a business professional who is completely grasped by the promise of wealth and status that rests at the top of the corporate ladder. His experience of the concern—its demand as well as its promise—is beyond a doubt. He feels it. It claims him, giving him purpose, driving him unflinchingly to climb upward until he realizes his goal.

Of course, whether the content or object of a person's ultimate concern can bring the fulfillment it promises remains an open question. Such is the risk of faith. "Only certain," Tillich writes, "is the ultimacy as ultimacy, the infinite passion as infinite passion. This is the reality given to the self with its own nature. It is as immediate and as much beyond doubt as the self is to the self. It *is* the self in its self-transcending quality" (*DF*, op. cit., p. 19; italics original). By "self-transcending quality" Tillich refers to the capacity of a human being—as distinct from other creatures—to rise above the immediacy of the present moment and define himself in light of who or what he values most in life. The risk of faith, therefore, does not refer to whether the individual believes in a God who may or may not exist. The risk of faith refers to whether the object of his faith has the ability to deliver what it promises—true fulfillment. If it does not, he worships a finite god and his faith is in vain. He surrenders his life to something that is ultimately not worth it. This is why Tillich refers to faith as the greatest risk a person can take, for if the devotee discovers he is wrong the meaning of his life falls apart. His god has failed.

When a person surrenders to something as a matter of ultimate concern, the "something" in question requires a symbol. For Tillich symbols are the language of faith. They provide faith with its "concrete content." Unfortunately, at least in matters pertaining to explicitly religious faith, people often equate the term "symbol" with a lesser truth or (at worst) a fairy tale. If a minister, for example, tells his congregation that the story of Adam and his expulsion from the Garden of Eden is not an event that took place in the past but a narrative symbolizing the most basic predicament of humankind (i.e., our separation from God), some members of his congregation may object. For them, the story is not "only a symbol" expressing humanity's separation from God. They believe it is a historical fact. Otherwise, it is not true. Here, because of what Tillich calls the "objectifying attitude" of modern people who think of truth in exclusively referential terms, the symbol of Adam's fall loses its ability to express a much deeper and *ultimate* insight into the human condition and its relation (or lack thereof) to God. It hardens into a stale belief a person must accept, one that unnecessarily contradicts science, all because the audience in question fails to understand the power of the symbol and the truth, as Tillich says, that "nothing less" than a symbol can convey" (*Ibid.*, p. 61).

So what truth do symbols of faith convey? What is their function and why does Tillich insist that nothing less than symbols can express a person or community's ultimate concern? The present chapter addresses these questions, showing why the proper understanding of a symbol's function and power as well as the corresponding need to interpret the contents of biblical faith in non-literal terms were among Tillich's highest priorities as a Christian theologian. Once we have summarized Tillich's view of symbols as the language of faith, we conclude the chapter by addressing a final question, the answer to which empowered Tillich to confront the nationalism of Nazi Germany as fundamentally demonic: How do we determine which among the pantheon of symbols expressing ultimate concern best and most effectively provides access to the true ultimate (i.e., God) over and against the lesser gods of idolatrous faith?

To make sense of how Tillich understands the function of symbols consider the distinction he draws between symbols and signs. Both of these convey meaning, and both point beyond themselves. Both represent or stand for something else. Signs, of course, are much more common in daily usage than symbols. The stop sign at the corner and the traffic light at an intersection are signs. However different these signs may be, their essential function remains the same. They direct the one interpreting the sign to a meaning beyond the sign itself. When a traffic light changes from green to red, for instance, it signifies a particular meaning to a driver. The meaning is simply a matter of social convention: no necessary connection exists between "red" and "stop," but so long as the convention (i.e., the arbitrarily agreed-upon meaning) remains in place the driver will (hopefully) make the connection in his mind.

Symbols have the same function. Like signs, Tillich says, "they point beyond themselves to something else" (*Ibid.*, p. 47). Yet symbols according to Tillich's analysis have an additional capacity that signs lack: "while the sign bears no relation to that to which it points, the symbol participates in the reality of that for which it stands" (*PTTB*, op cit., p. 166). Our theologian's wording may sound strange, but his point is actually simple. Consider the following example: if a person vandalizes a stop sign he obviously breaks the law, but he probably does nothing to violate a community's sensibilities or create controversy. This is because the stop sign is just a sign. If the same person burns an American flag, on the other hand, imagine the response he might receive! Here we see the basic difference between a sign and a symbol. Both point to or convey a meaning beyond themselves, but only the symbol (the flag) "participates" in the power or reality which it represents. This "power" is that which people experience as something greater than themselves. It grasps human beings through the concrete medium of a particular symbol or set of symbols which is why Tillich calls symbols the language of faith. They enable people to be grasped by something that concerns them ultimately.

Tillich directly employs the example of a nation's flag in his description of symbols and what they do: "the flag participates in the power and dignity of the nation for which it stands" (*DF*, op. cit., p. 48). This fact helps us understand why the United States government has come close to passing legislation that would make flag-burning illegal. Such effort reveals clearly the enormous power of a symbol in contrast to mere signs. "An attack on the flag," Tillich explains, "is felt as an attack on the majesty of the group in which it is acknowledged. Such an attack is considered blasphemy" (*Ibid*). Perhaps the best example in recent memory of the power symbols have to express a group's ultimate concern appears in the tragedy of 9-11. In planning their attack, members of al-Queda obviously chose targets of symbolic value to Americans. Had they destroyed a random target without symbolic value their plot would have had much less of an impact on the American populace. Instead, they aimed right at the heart of America's faith in free-market capitalism and militaristic power as symbolized by the World Trade Center and the Pentagon, respectively, causing fear and anger of immense proportions. This, as in the prior case of flag burning, discloses the power of symbols as distinct from signs.

Whether one places one's trust or absolute confidence for the sake of fulfillment in a nation, an economic system, the

God of a particular religion, another person, or in wealth, the fact remains that symbols give each of these potential deities its concrete content; through symbols each of these powers can claim individuals as well as large groups of people. Symbols, therefore, are indispensible to faith. The flag, the World Trade Center, the cross, and the swastika represent concerns that become matters of life and death for those who find themselves in their grasp. This is not to say these symbols will always function as symbols, much less that we can produce them intentionally. Indeed, they have a life of their own: "They grow out of the individual or collective unconscious and cannot function without being accepted by the unconscious dimension of our being" (*Ibid.*, p. 49). When they do appear, however, they can dramatically change the course of a person's life.

When a symbol appears the power it conveys can also change the life and circumstances of an entire population. But like the population itself, symbols do not endure forever. They grow, they live, and they die. By saying that a symbol lives Tillich means that it has the capacity to elicit a faith response. The cross of Christ, for example, remains a living symbol insofar as it has the ability to elicit a faith response from millions of people even today. Dead symbols, by contrast, no longer have such power. Their carcasses line the dusty road of human history, extending back through the gods of Rome, Greece, and Egypt to the pre-historic cave-drawings of Chauvet in France and El Castillo in northern Spain. Part of what determines a symbol's adequacy to point toward the true ultimate, therefore, depends on whether it is alive, that is, whether it has the ability to grasp an individual or a group by drawing people out of themselves and orienting them toward "something more."

Symbols tell us something, then, about who we are as humans. They reveal a spiritual disposition we have toward something greater than ourselves, toward a wholeness from which (Tillich says) we are separated and for which we yearn. By providing access to this dimension of being, symbols can be an avenue through which individuals experience and receive transformation and healing. Tillich cites the experience of the Apostle Paul as an example:

> In the picture of Jesus as the Christ, which appeared to him at the moment of his greatest separation from other men, from himself and God, he found himself accepted in spite of his being rejected. And when he found that he was accepted, he was able to accept himself and to be reconciled to others. The moment in which grace struck him and overwhelmed him, he was reunited with that to which he belonged, and from which he was estranged in utter strangeness (*SF*, op. cit., p. 160).

This "picture," the manifestation of an image Paul encountered, was and has since become a powerful symbol that has transformed the lives of many people. As a symbol it mediates what Tillich considers to be the power of healing—in the case of Paul, the power of acceptance and reconciliation—that enabled him "to accept himself and to be reconciled to others."

Symbols can also communicate a destructive power, one that Tillich describes as the "form-destroying" eruption of the demonic in history. The source of this power is nonbeing which, at least as it subsists within God, is neither good nor bad. (We will discuss the nature of nonbeing more fully later.) The transition from nonbeing in God to what Tillich calls the form-destroying power of the demonic in history is triggered, however, by idolatrous faith. Remember here that symbols provide access to the sacred dimension of all being. Their task is to point beyond themselves. The test of a symbol's truth revolves around how adequately it expresses ultimate concern, how well it puts one in touch with the truly sacred. Unfortunately, Tillich observes, many symbols of faith fail in their task. Instead of pointing to the true ultimate, they claim ultimacy for themselves. When this happens faith becomes idolatrous.

The problem with idolatrous faith, as noted, is its destructive or form-destroying power. The moment people claim to possess truth for themselves through their primary symbol or symbols of faith, the power that (in fact) *possesses them* often leads to intolerance and even the persecution of others who see matters differently. When this happens the faith in question has become absolutist and demonic. History contains many examples, particularly in the twentieth century, of idolatrous faith and its destructive power. The source of this faith is sin: the human mind, estranged from its divine source, reflects its "fallenness" by investing symbols for the divine with divinity themselves. "The weakness of faith," Tillich writes, "is the ease with which it becomes idolatrous. The human mind, Calvin has said, is a continuously working factory of idols" (*DF*, op. cit., p. 111). Idolatry is a frequent temptation.

What people need if they desire access to the true ultimate, then, is a symbol that negates itself so that the rays of divine light can break through the clouds of estrangement with their form-fulfilling or life-giving power. The symbol must be transparent. It must be a window to the sacred, not a wall. It must resist the attempt to obstruct true ultimacy by claiming ultimacy for itself. To do this it must negate or "break" itself in the name of the ultimate for which it stands; otherwise, it becomes an idol to which people devote themselves rather than an icon through which people access the sacred. Next to a symbol's ability to grasp human beings by eliciting a faith response, therefore, Tillich considers the final test of its adequacy to be its ability to point beyond itself by negating itself. Not surprisingly, he derives this test of a symbol's adequacy from the center of his own religious tradition—the cross of Jesus the Christ.

While many Catholic and Protestant Christians interpret the crucifixion of Jesus as a sacrifice he made to pay for the sins of humankind, Tillich sees the sacrificial character of Jesus' death in another way. For him it marks the culmination of a story in which Jesus of Nazareth, the one through whom his followers found themselves grasped by a sacred power beyond themselves, faces and overcomes the demonic temptation to claim this power as his own. This, Tillich argues, makes him the ultimate symbol for God: he provides others with access to God while simultaneously resisting the opportunity to "seize" the nature of God for himself (Philippians 2:5-8); he insists that no one—not even he—is good but God alone (Mark 10:18); he rejects the devil's offer to be like God (Matthew 4:1-11); and he claims that those who believe in him believe not in him but in the Father who sent him (John 12:44). In his death on the cross his victorious refusal to be worshipped in the place of God finds definitive symbolic expression, providing what Tillich regards as the ultimate criterion by which to judge "the truth of faith" (*Ibid.*, p. 110f; *ST*, vol. 2., op. cit., p. 126). As the Christ he cancels himself out, and in the process provides access through himself to God.

Here again we must pause. If Jesus is the Christ insofar as he negates himself while remaining a living symbol through which people can access the radiating light of being-itself or, in more traditional terms, if he is a mediator between God and humanity who makes it possible to access the sacred in a non-idolatrous way, does this mean that he is "only" a symbol? The answer to this question is two-fold.

First, remember that for Tillich symbols point beyond themselves to something else. In speaking of something literally, by contrast, we assume a direct correspondence between a word and the object or reality to which the word refers. It makes sense to use literal language if one can point directly to an object—a cup on a table or a computer on a desk—and name it. But, in the tradition of the Catholic theologian St. Thomas Aquinas, Tillich insists that God is not simply an object like a cup or a computer. Literal language for God accordingly does not suffice: to speak of God in the same way one speaks of a cup or a computer objectifies God, reducing

God to a thing among things. This is why Tillich says that "[l]iteralism deprives God of his ultimacy and, religiously speaking, of his majesty. It draws him down to the level of that which is not ultimate, the finite and the conditional" (*DF*, op. cit., p. 60). Symbols, by contrast, provide an alternative to literal language for God insofar as they can point beyond themselves to a dimension beyond space and time without objectifying that to which they point. They evoke without encapsulating.

The best example of what happens when people take a religious symbol literally appears in the language for God as "father." If we use the term literally, Tillich implies, we mean that God is fundamentally no different than a human father. Granted, He may be bigger and more powerful than an ordinary man, but direct, one-to-one correspondence otherwise remains: as in the case of a father, God has a tangible body with physical features. Unfortunately, speaking of God literally as a father reduces God to "a being besides others and as such a part of the whole of reality. He certainly is considered to be its most important part, but as a part and therefore as subjected to the structure of the whole" (*CTB*, op. cit., p. 184). On the other hand, if we understand the language of Father symbolically with respect to God, we recognize the truth of the symbol (i.e., we experience God as having fatherly characteristics, say, insofar as God constitutes the source of our being) without reducing God (as in the case of literalism) to a being or an actual human father. This is why Tillich insists that we should use *nothing less than a symbol* in reference to God.

We will return to a fuller explanation of Tillich's view of God in the next two chapters. For now this point should be clear: Tillich's conviction that only symbolic language can adequately point to God or express ultimate concern does not deny the reality of God. It denies the capacity of human language, directly or literally, to name God. That said, since God (i.e., being-itself) and human beings share being in common, we can speak analogously, symbolically or indirectly about who and what God is. We can say God is like a father or has fatherly characteristics without limiting God to an actual father. While some people, including the "death of God" theologian Paul van Buren and the philosopher Ludwig Wittgenstein, would assert that no language—literal or symbolic—could name or even point to God since "God" is not a referent, Tillich's most ardent detractors were and are biblical literalists who defend literal language for God because "the Bible tells them so." What they fail to understand, Tillich says, is that their literalism ultimately undermines the divinity of God.

When a person reads the Bible she can approach it in at least one of two ways. She can assume, as modern biblical literalists do, that something is true based upon whether it happened. In this case, Tillich writes:

> Christianity defends itself, but in doing so it unconsciously moves on the same level against which it would defend itself—the level of mere objectification. It turns the symbolic stories of biblical literature into objectified events. It does what it should fight against. This makes the situation extremely difficult. In centuries in which this objectification had not yet taken place, or not yet grasped most people, myth, legend, and history were mixed. There was no real difference between them, and a miracle story was not more difficult to accept than a so-called historical story. But in the moment that the modern mind realized the difference of history, legend, and myth—and efforts were made to defend the biblical stories as objectively demonstrable—the Christian case was lost. The defenders had surrendered their defensive power (*IR*, op. cit., pp. 36-37).

The reason Tillich says "the Christian case was lost" is that many of its defenders turned faith into a set of beliefs that people must accept on the same terms as they would accept the truths of scientific fact. Before the modern era, however, nobody denied the reality of miracles on the basis of their interference with scientific laws. Occasional critics would reject the belief in miracles as an expression of superstition, but the general populace simply accepted their occurrence as part of the pre-scientific world in which they lived. When Jesus performs "deeds of power" according to the Gospels, for example, his challengers never ask *how* he did them; they merely desire to know by whose authority (see Luke 20:2).

The defense of biblical stories as "objectively demonstrable" creates the most harm when it comes to how we understand God. When people take stories of or relating to God in Scripture as literal descriptions about God, they reduce God to a being, "acting in time and space, dwelling in a special place, affecting the course of events and being affected by them like any other being in the universe" (*DF*, op. cit., p. 59). Imagining God as a being who periodically intervenes in the course of history obviously means nothing to people whose view of the universe has been shaped by science; beyond that, Tillich also finds this version of God theologically offensive. How can God, who supposedly structures and grounds all being, be a speck of being in the realm of being? What a puny God!

The alternative, says Tillich, is to interpret talk about God in the Bible symbolically. The question, then, is not whether something about divine action in the Bible is true, but how it is true—not whether something happened, but what something means in reference to the nature of ultimate reality. What *ultimate* truth, in other words, does the story under consideration convey symbolically? Once again we return to the beginning: when God expels Adam and Eve from the Garden of Eden for transgressing God's will, the question (from Tillich's point of view) should not be whether this event happened *once upon a time*. The question should be: What might the narrative tell us about who we are in relation to God? What insight does it contain about our predicament of separation from God or about our ongoing tendency to elevate ourselves to the status of God *all the time*? The point, in short, is to "de-literalize" Scripture so that it can speak to us through its symbols and stories at the deepest level of our being.

Does the attempt to de-literalize Scripture suggest, then, that we can eventually abandon the symbols of biblical religion altogether once we have gleaned from them the enduring truths about God, morality, or the human condition which they contain? Tillich's answer is "no." While we should recognize the symbols in Scripture as symbols, we must retain these symbols and myths (by which Tillich simply means collections of symbols in narrative form). This is because "nothing less" than symbols—especially the technical-empirical language of science—can express ultimate concern; the symbols of biblical religion must all be preserved and constantly reinterpreted, therefore, to meet the ever-changing situation in which human beings find themselves. This gives the Christian message its lasting relevance, so long as pastors and theologians of each new generation make the attempt to interpret the symbols of Scripture in ways that actually speak to the predicament of the audience or audiences they are addressing. (This also does not mean that some of the symbols—particularly the cross of Christ—were not historical events; it means, however, that we miss the point when we think being Christian means defending the symbols as literal truths instead of mining them for meaning and insight regarding *ultimate* truth.)

To summarize: Nothing less than symbols can communicate the truth of faith. This is because they point beyond themselves to God without making God into a being. "Although symbols, for Tillich, are always constrained and finite," as the Tillich scholar Andrew O'Neill points out, "they are never 'merely' symbols, because that to which they refer is unconstrained and infinite" (*Tillich: A Guide for the Perplexed*, T&T Clark, 2008, p. 23). Apart from their capacity to point beyond themselves, symbols also share in the reality to which they point. This is crucial to remember when Tillich speaks of Christ as a symbol for God. Critics of Tillich's Christology (i.e., his understanding of who Jesus was as the Christ) almost invariably overlook the participatory nature of symbols. Jesus as the Christ is not "only" a symbol; he *shares* in the truly ultimate power to which he points by negating himself as an object of worship. He becomes the one through whom Paul in his letters repeatedly prays to God as well the one through whom God has reconciled the world to himself (2 Corinthians 5:19). In more traditional terminology, he is the mediator between God and humanity who makes what Tillich, again following the Apostle Paul, refers to as the "new reality" available to people who find themselves grasped by the life-giving power working through him.

Tillich's depitction of "Jesus the crucified" as the ultimate symbol for God helps us perceive the basis, finally, for his critique of Nazism as the face of "demonic powers . . . that destroy nation and humanity" (*PTTB*, op. cit., p. 118). These powers, Tillich writes in 1932, must be subjected to the judgment of the cross: "Protestantism must prove its prophetic-Christian character by setting the Christianity of the cross against the paganism of the swastika. Protestantism must testify that the cross has broken and judged the 'holiness' of nation, race, blood, and power" (*Ibid.*, p. 117). A horde of dangerous idols, Tillich says to his contemporaries, has taken the place of God, claiming ultimacy and holiness for themselves. This is the demonic power of idolatrous faith. Unfortunately, those who heard or read Tillich's words did not heed them. Less than a decade after Tillich wrote what he did the powers he named had seized an entire nation, bringing about precisely what Tillich had foreseen: the nation's own destruction and with it the obliteration of millions of innocent people.

Of course, Tillich also knew that that idolatry was a constant temptation of Christians who likewise stood under the judgment of the cross. Whenever people of Christian faith make something finite into God, including the Church (as in late medieval Roman Catholicism), the Bible (as in seventeenth century Lutheranism or contemporary Christian fundamentalism), or even Jesus himself (as in Jesusolatry), they block the true God from view. Even "God," Tillich concludes, "is a symbol for God" (*DF*, op. cit., p. 53). This is because God transcends God's own name, as the story of Moses' first encounter with God (Exodus 3:14) confirms: God has no name. God is not a being one can name; God is being-itself. Yet by saying God is being-itself, have we not directly named God, and what does being-itself actually mean? To answer these questions we turn next to the gleaming star at the center of Tillich's theology: his doctrine of God as being-itself.

CHAPTER SIX

GOD

Religious symbols, we have now seen, express faith. They orient us to something greater than ourselves, to an ultimate dimension of being that transcends the structure of ordinary, finite reality. Yet the symbols of faith available to human beings are far from being equal. The one most adequate to its task not only puts people in touch with a reality greater than itself by eliciting a faith response; it negates itself as a potential object of worship in the process. This allows for the kind of non-idolatrous faith that makes spiritual healing possible, reconnecting human beings with the true ultimate (God) from which they have been estranged and to which they essentially belong. While Tillich leaves open the possibility that symbols of varying religious faiths can function in self-negating, non-idolatrous ways, he maintains as a Christian theologian that the supreme expression of a non-idolatrous symbol appears in the image of Christ-crucified. This is the ultimate basis of the Protestant Principle: in the sacrifice of Jesus as Jesus he becomes the mediator between God and humanity, making the sacred available to others through him by *taking up his cross and denying himself* as the object of devotion.

Tillich's view of symbols as the language of faith invariably raises the question of why God remains inaccessible to language in its ordinary, direct, or literal form. The reason, as we indicated in the previous chapter, is that God, the timeless mystery and depth-dimension of being, "transcends the realm of finite reality infinitely. Therefore, no finite reality can express it directly and properly" (*Ibid.*, p. 51). God resides beyond our conceptual and linguistic grasp because God is not an object, a person, or a speck of being. Only symbols can make God available to human beings. They are absolutely indispensable for providing access to God. Yet they must be recognized as symbols. If people take symbols for God literally, they "draw him down to the level of that which is not ultimate, the finite and conditional" (*Ibid.*, p. 60). Thus while the ultimate aim or referent of symbolic language is God, and while nothing less than a symbol can mediate or make available God's presence to human beings, God is not a being. God is being-itself.

Tillich develops his understanding of God as being-itself in the first of what would become his three-volume *Systematic Theology*. Tillich derives the term "being-itself," which he baptizes in the service of Christian faith, from his former colleague at the University of Marburg, the philosopher Martin Heidegger. According to Tillich being-itself is the only literal description one can apply to God. He writes, "The statement that God is being-itself is a non-symbolic statement. It does not point beyond itself. It means what it says directly and properly; if we speak of the actuality of God, we first assert that he is not God if he is not being itself" (*ST*, vol. 1., op. cit., pp. 238-239). Tillich also accepts the term "power of being," which we have mentioned in previous chapters, as a corollary (though metaphorical) expression: since being-itself "points to the power inherent in everything, the power to resist nonbeing," the phrase "power of being" can likewise refer to God (*Ibid.*, p. 236).

Tillich's refusal to identify God as an entity, object or being amounts to a startling revelation: God does not exist. To say that God exists is to pair together what Tillich refers to as an impossible or meaningless combination of words. Here the reader should pause: Why would a Christian theologian deny the existence of God? Was Tillich an atheist or a proponent of the "death of God" theology that became popular later in the 1960s? Did he reject "the reality, the validity, the truth of the idea of God" (as he puts it) or was he challenging a misconception of God? To arrive at an answer, this chapter summarizes

Tillich's understanding of God as being-itself insofar as the term relates to the question of whether God actually exists. It illustrates how Tillich avoids reducing God to a being or person while preserving at the same time an understanding of God that includes a personal component, one that arguably makes possible a relationship with God in personal terms. The chapter concludes by showing how Tillich is at once both innovative and traditional in his doctrine of God, how for him God is real even though God does not literally "exist."

Few people, of course, think of God explicitly as being-itself! Nevertheless, Tillich writes, "even in the most primitive intuition of the divine a feeling should be, and usually is, present that there is a mystery about divine names which makes them improper, self-transcending, symbolic" (*Ibid.*, p. 242). In other words, people instinctively know that their language falls short when it comes to naming God, that the divine mystery remains a target that lies well beyond human speech and concepts. Perhaps we can name "toward" God, as the Catholic theologian Elizabeth Johnson puts it, but we can never name God as such. Words fail. For Tillich this is not simply because we need to make more of an effort; it is because no direct correspondence exists (with the exception of "being-itself") between our words for God and God as such since God is not an object in space and time.

The intuition that God lies beyond our linguistic grasp finds its confirmation biblically in the "name" by which God refers to Godself according to the author of Exodus 3:14. When Moses asks God for God's identity, the latter replies with the pithy term for existence-itself in Hebrew: "I am," or as the medieval theologian Meister Eckhart translates it, "I am being." Here we have what Tillich might regard as the most sublime description of God in the Old Testament. While other biblical texts depict God in anthropomorphic terms (i.e., as a person-like figure or being), Tillich contends that "prophetic utterances in the Old Testament" implicitly resist the reduction of God to an existing subject in the order of temporal reality. Even though they use concrete language for God rather than the abstraction of being-itself, they "never make God a being alongside others, into something conditioned by something else which is also conditioned" (*Ibid*). Instead, they stress the absolute transcendence of God in symbolic terms. The task of the theologian, in turn, is neither to negate nor confirm these and other symbols for ultimate reality in the Bible, but "to interpret them according to theological principles and methods" (*Ibid*., p. 240).

So how does Tillich interpret symbolically a passage in the Bible where the author clearly depicts God anthropomorphically? The answer is this: when a biblical text like Isaiah 6:1 speaks, for example, of God sitting on a throne in heaven, we have to ask *what such language means*. If we interpret it to mean that God, a person, literally and spatially resides somewhere "up in the heavens on an ethereal cloud," as the journalist Ed Briggs put it several years after Tillich's death, we obviously and unnecessarily contradict contemporary science, not to mention the fact that we also (yet again) reduce God to a being. On the other hand, if we interpret such language symbolically we can see that it points to the absolute transcendence of God, which is to say that God "exists" not simply beyond the world geographically, but beyond (or better, beneath) space and time altogether. Here we have another example of why Tillich insists that we must "de-literalize" language for God in Scripture: locating God literally and spatially in a realm above the clouds makes God into a mere being among beings rather than the timeless depth and power of being as such.

Emphasis on the timelessness and complete transcendence of God, one that commonly falls under the label of "classical theism," finds expression in the Christian tradition as early as the second and third centuries of the Common Era. Yet, as much as Tillich reflects the classical theism of his Christian and Jewish forbears, he also departs from them in at least two significant ways: first, he incorporates into his view a theological sub-tradition that identifies God *not as person but as a process* which (Tillich insists) somehow resolves itself outside of time. Second, he identifies God with the always-active power that continuously generates and sustains material being, the "stuff" of our world and the universe. In the next chapter we will turn to a fuller analysis of how Tillich elaborates upon and includes these two notions in his theology. For now, our journey through the labyrinth of his doctrine of God begins by examining the claim he made that inspired some of his mid-twentieth century contemporaries to label him "the most dangerous theologian alive": God does not exist.

To think of God as non-existent amounts to what most people would consider conventional atheism. Yet Tillich maintains throughout his writings as a Christian theologian that God does not literally exist. He explains his position as follows:

> If "existence" refers to something which can be found in the whole of reality, no divine being exists. The question is not this, but: which of the innumerable symbols of faith is most adequate to the meaning of faith? In other words, which symbol of ultimacy expresses the ultimacy without idolatrous elements? This is the problem, and not the so-called "existence of God"—which is in itself an impossible combination of words (*DF*, op. cit., p. 54).

Tillich's observation that the "existence of God" is an "impossible combination of words" comes from his awareness regarding the original meaning of the term "exist" in Latin: namely, to stand out or emerge from something else. If God is God, the argument goes, God cannot exist as we do because God is the source and power of being—the "something else" out of which we stand and from which we derive our being. "He is being-itself," Tillich explains, "beyond essence [being in its potential form] and existence [being in its actual form]. Therefore to argue that God exists is to deny him" (*ST*, vol. 1., op. cit., p. 239).

Let us consider Tillich's argument more closely. To say that God exists is to affirm that God is distinct from the source of being, that God depends on a reality other than God for God's own existence, or that God is subject to something greater than Godself—the totality of reality or, as Tillich puts it, "the structure of being" (*Ibid.*, p. 238). But if God is God, should not God be "the ground of the structure of being," the source, depth, and power from whom all beings receive their being? If not, if God "exists" or stands out as *a* being and receives God's being from another source, then do those who claim to worship God actually worship the great "I am" of Exodus 3:14, the true ultimate in whom "we live and move and have our being" (Acts 17:28)? Or do they subscribe to what Tillich calls "monarchic monotheism" which subordinates God (understood as a supreme being, king, or ruler) to the source of being (i.e., being-itself) "just as Zeus is subordinate to fate in Greek religion" (*Ibid.*, p. 236)? These are the tough questions Tillich puts to the faithful among his readership, not in an effort to deny God, but to preserve—as he sees it—God's "ultimacy and, religiously speaking . . . his majesty" (*DF*, op. cit., p. 60).

Tillich is no less merciful on the critics of religion. Those who reject what they assume to be a divine being "out there," the existence or non-existence of which can be determined by empirical observation, are not rejecting God in the Christian—or at least Tillichian—sense. God does not exist as an entity or being who stands out from the depth and radiating power of being-itself; God *is* this depth and power. If the critic of religion wishes to reject the reality or truth of God, therefore, he should (according to Tillich) target the ideas of its strongest representatives instead of meddling with the inadequate notions of God to which only some in the faith tradition subscribe.

While Tillich remains critical of those who fail "to attack the most advanced and not some obsolete form of [theology]" (*TC*, op. cit., p. 129), he praises the constructive role atheism can generally play in refining the way people of religious faith think about God. The reason is simple: atheism helps to eradicate deficient views of God. It purifies and refines the content of faith by denying the existence of God perceived as a being so that the sunrise of being-itself (i.e., the source and power of being or what Tillich calls the "God above God" in *The Courage to Be*) can emerge from behind the horizon of objectified theism in all its splendor and theological glory. In other words, atheism rightly rejects the existence of a personal God or gods, at least literally understood. Tillich writes:

> The concept of a "Personal God," interfering with natural events, or being "an independent cause of natural events," makes God a natural object beside others, an object among objects, a being among beings, maybe the highest, but nevertheless *a* being. This, indeed, is the destruction . . . of any meaningful idea of God. . . . No criticism of this distorted idea of God can be sharp enough (*Ibid.*, p. 130).

While some—including the "new" atheist Richard Dawkins—might respond by saying they deny not only the interventionist God Tillich describes here, but any version of God or reality greater than our own, there are others who, upon reflection, might nod approvingly in Tillich's direction. One such person is Albert Einstein.

Einstein gave a talk just before the middle of the twentieth century in which he repudiated the existence of a personal God. Tillich wrote a response which began with a summary of Einstein's argument. According to Tillich, Einstein basically argues that the concept of a personal God "contradicts the scientific interpretation of nature" (*Ibid.*, p. 129). Theologians and other people of religious faith who believe in a personal God who interferes with the course of natural events to explain them undermine legitimate scientific inquiry. Tillich agrees. "Theology," he writes, "must leave to science the description of the whole of objects and their interdependence in nature and history, in man and his world" (*Ibid*). This is because, we recall, science and religion speak to two different realms of being—being in the arena of space and time (science) and being at its depth and ground (religion).

Interestingly enough, the argument that belief in God should not interfere with the scientific interpretation of nature does not exhaust what Einstein says on the topic. While the great physicist rejects the existence of a personal God, he speaks favorably of a disposition toward the heart of nature in a way that closely resembles Tillich's description of faith: "the true scientist 'attains that humble attitude of mind toward the grandeur of reason incarnate in existence, which, in its profoundest depths is inaccessible to man'" (Tillich quoted Einstein, *ibid*., p. 130). The parallel is not lost on Tillich. He writes:

> If we interpret these words rightly, they point to a common ground of the whole physical world and its suprapersonal values; a ground which, on the one hand, is manifest in the structure of being (the physical world) and meaning (the good, true, and beautiful), and which, on the other hand, is hidden in its inexhaustible depth (*Ibid*).

All existence, in other words, has its root in a "depth" inaccessible to human beings. This depth marks what Tillich calls the divine ground of being which, as in the case of Einstein, inspires the feeling and experience of (holy) awe and wonder that religion attempts to cultivate in the context of community. "But since it [the depth] is 'inaccessible' to any objectifying concept," Tillich adds, "it must be expressed in symbols" (*Ibid*., p. 131). The most common symbol for doing so in religion is that of the personal God.

Tillich's critics usually reject his view of God as too impersonal and abstract. For this reason we must consider what he says here about the symbol of a personal God carefully. Remember first that to interpret the symbol of a personal God literally is to reduce God to a person which makes God into a being. This is undesirable. It limits God by turning God into something conditioned by a greater totality. At the same time, to speak of God as impersonal is to make God less than human. But if the phenomenon of personhood is something we derive from God, the source and foundation of our existence, it stands to reason that this source and foundation—which is greater than we are—would include the personal within itself. The symbol of a personal God points, in turn, to the dimension of the personal within the matrix of being-itself without reducing being-itself to a person. This makes the depth of existence "suprapersonal" (Einstein) or "transpersonal" (Tillich), not impersonal. To use the symbol of a personal God for this sacred depth, Tillich explains, "does not mean that God is a person. It means that God is the ground of everything personal and that he carries within him the ontological power of personality. He is not a person, but he is not less than personal" (*ST*, vol. 1, op. cit., p. 245).

By locating the personal within God while resisting the temptation to make God into a person (and thereby limiting God), Tillich preserves the possibility of affirming the experience of God as personal through the *symbol* of a personal God. This symbol enables people of religious faith to enjoy communion with God in personal terms by making accessible the personal dimension of being-itself. If we interpret the symbol literally (i.e., if we reduce the personal within God which we experience through the symbol to a person or a being), then Einstein's criticism stands. But if we can relate to God through it we can be "grasped [at] the center of our personality" and healed of our anxiety, loneliness, and despair. Tillich writes, "Acceptance by something which is less than personal could not overcome personal self-rejection. A wall to which I confess cannot forgive me. No self-acceptance is possible if one is not accepted in a person-to-person relation" (*CTB*, op. cit., p. 166). Only God experienced in personal, relational terms can become for us an ultimate concern, an object of faith, a reason for being, a guide for our lives, a source of comfort in times of trial, or the basis of courage in the midst of adversity. The symbol of a personal God allows us to experience God in a personal way even though God is infinitely more than a person.

Tillich's view of God in "super-personal" terms undeniably constitutes one of the most difficult concepts in his theology. His basic point is this: nobody can have a relationship with an abstraction or pray to being-itself. Such language is eminently useful in second-order theological reflection, but in the first-order language of personal faith or worship it has little (if any) place. While the terminology of "depth" or "ground" may inspire awe and wonder, Tillich maintains that religion in practice rightly employs the symbol of a personal God so that people, in relation to the personal dimension of divine reality embedded within the matrix and depth of divine being, can encounter God in an existentially significant manner. Through the symbol of a personal God, in other words, people can relate to God as an "eternal thou" or "you." Only in this way can a human being be claimed or "grasped" by the healing power of the divine (i.e., grace or acceptance), a point to which we will return shortly.

For the moment we must pause to consider an important question: Why is being-itself not directly available to human experience? Why does ultimate reality have to be mediated to us through symbols? If God is all-powerful, could not God simply part the clouds and descend from heaven for all to see? The answer (yet again) is that being-itself is not an object or person. To suggest that a direct experience of God is possible automatically reduces the divine—which is present in, with, and under all things—to a being. While we can experience this God through symbols (or through a "mediator," to use more traditional language), and while we can argue that God contains the phenomenon of the personal within Godself which is made available to us through symbols like "God the Father," we cannot suggest that God might appear to us literally as an object or person somewhere "out there" in the field of ordinary vision. God becomes manifest to us, rather, through things—"mythological symbols and theological concepts, ritual and sacrament, demands for social justice, and even the honesty of scientific investigation," as O'Neill puts it—not as *a thing* (O'Neill, op. cit., p. 20).

Should one desire to access God directly in another way apart from experience, say by using reason or deducing "proofs" for the existence of God, Tillich has more bad news: rational arguments for God's existence also fail. They all rest on the assumption that, starting with some aspect of existence like the apparent order or "design" of nature, human logic can "make the conclusion 'God' necessary" (*ST*, vol. 1., op. cit., p. 205). Unfortunately, as O'Neill points out regarding Tillich's view, "the logical need for an unmoved mover [i.e., God as the "big bang" of first cause of the universe] does not guarantee its existence" (O'Neill, op. cit., p. 62). "Proofs" for God's existence, moreover, reduce God to the level of finite reality, making God a cause in the order of being rather than preserving God's status as being-itself. "[I]f we derive God from the world," Tillich explains, "he cannot be that which transcends the world infinitely" (*ST*, vol. 1, op. cit., p. 205).

What "evidence," then, do human beings have for the reality or truth of God? Popular arguments for God's "existence" apparently fail, and human experience cannot directly encounter or verify the reality of God without symbolic mediation since God is not a being or a finite cause "out there." Where can a person turn? The answer, says Tillich, is in the question itself—the question of God. The question of God presupposes an "awareness" of the infinite! The infinite is something of which people are implicitly aware when they raise the question of God. Their minds intuitively grasp what it is even though no object or experience in our finite reality corresponds to it. Why is that? From where do we obtain this intuition if not from an innate familiarity with the infinite or what Tillich usually calls "the unconditioned" itself (i.e., God)?

For Tillich our innate or intuitive awareness of the infinite (which again the question of God presupposes) stems from the fact that we share or "participate" in the timelessness of being-itself insofar as we have being. Obviously the being we have is limited and finite because we "stand out" from being-itself; yet we also participate in being-itself which has no limitation. This is because, as we will explain next chapter, being has overcome nonbeing eternally in God. The absolute victory of being over nonbeing in God frees being-itself of all limitation which makes it infinite. Our participation in the limitlessness of being-itself explains why we have an intuitive awareness of the infinite which religion, in turn, names as God, providing the infinite with its "concrete content" through symbols.

Verifying the reality of the infinite through the interior awareness we have of it instead of trying to prove the existence of God based on the external observation of nature or the universe (as in the method of arguments from "design") reflects a procedure that extends back to St. Augustine, one which Tillich explicitly endorses in his 1946 essay, "The Two Types of Philosophy of Religion." After Augustine the approach resurfaces again in the writings of the philosopher Descartes who argues, as Tillich points out, that "the infinite in our minds presupposes the infinite itself" (*TC*, op. cit., p. 128). In the nineteenth century it appears once more in the writings of Friedrich Schleiermacher who takes as his point of departure for theological reflection what he considers to be the universal, pre-linguistic feeling of dependence human beings have on "something greater" than themselves. In the twentieth century the approach finds articulation most notably in the work of the Jesuit theologian Karl Rahner who speaks of an "unthematized" or pre-linguistic awareness of God native to human beings which religion makes conscious to its practitioners through symbols and language. While each of these perspectives differs with regard to important details, they share in a single conviction: the best argument for the reality of God is the given orientation of the human being toward "something more," and with it an intuitive pre-linguistic awareness of "the infinite."

The innate orientation human beings have toward something beyond ourselves as well as their implicit longing for it provides the basis for why Tillich encourages his audience (as we saw in chapter three) to ask ultimate questions. Questions of ultimacy enrich and reinforce the disposition human beings have toward something greater, preparing them to receive answers as mediated through religious symbols. Unfortunately, the awareness of the infinite to which we belong also constitutes the basis for why we experience anxiety in a way that other animals do not. Our consciousness is not bound to the immediate present. We have an awareness of the infinite to which we belong even though we do not own it like a possession. We know we are going to die, and so we experience anxiety which the symbols of faith (at least ideally) are meant to address.

The fact that human beings can legitimately raise the question of God puts Tillich in opposition to the most important Protestant theologian of the twentieth century, Karl Barth, who we mentioned when discussing Tillich's life in Germany. For Barth, human beings have no ability cognitively to approach God due to sin. People are so hopelessly lost that they cannot even raise the question of God. Barth's position has significant precedent in Paul (Romans 1:18-23) as well as in the writings of Luther, the latter of whom referred to reason, when misapplied to matters divine, as the devil's whore. This is because reason, like the body, was infected by the power of sin that Adam unleashed into the world in his fall from God (see Romans 5:12). Now that human beings are fundamentally out for themselves, the argument goes, they think in ways that tell us everything about their own self-interest and nothing about the God of Jesus Christ. Tillich was certainly sympathetic to the conviction that reason has its limits. He also maintains that sin, understood as estrangement or separation from God, prevents us from saving ourselves, yet he insists that for salvation to be meaningful it must address human beings in ways that correspond to their actual predicament. They must desire it. They must be able to ask for it. The Christian message, if it is effective, will meet this longing and (however fragmentarily) fulfill and heal it, but it has to do so in a way that meets people where they are. Correlating the questions of the modern period to their "answers" constitutes, in turn, the method that underlies Tillich's three-volume *Systematic Theology*.

Treating properly the scope of Tillich's *Systematic Theology* lies well beyond the confines of the present discussion. The important point to consider is this: in all three volumes of his *magnum opus*, Tillich presumes that God meets us where we are. He insists that we can at least ask the question of God even though, as O'Neill summarizes Tillich, "God's choice to reveal Godself to fallen humanity is an act of grace" (O'Neill, op. cit., p. 35). The restlessness, yearning and desire for completion and fulfillment inherent to human nature find their resolution in God. Human reason, which seeks unity with the truth from which it has been estranged, is met and fulfilled by divine revelation; the brokenness of human existence is met and healed in and through the "new being" of Jesus as the Christ; and the ambiguities of life, especially what Tillich calls "the inseparable mixture of good and evil," are met and addressed in relation to the divine Spirit (Taylor, *PTTB*, op. cit., p. 24f). In each of these cases, Tillich draws on various symbols of biblical faith (God, Christ, and the Holy Spirit) and interprets them in ways that address the conflicts inherent in human existence due to our estrangement from God. Through these symbols the power of being is mediated to human beings, providing them with the courage to face the difficulties and problems that belong to them as finite creatures constantly threatened by the negativities and insecurities they experience in life.

If symbols, then, make manifest the power of being to people in order to address and heal their existential conflicts and longings, what exactly do they reveal about God? What do they disclose about the properties or characteristics of being-itself? To clear the deck for a thorough answer, the present chapter has shown how Tillich emphasizes the need first to distinguish between God as being-itself from God as merely a being. The latter, Tillich argues, does not literally exist. God does not derive God's being or "stand out" from something else. God is the "something else" out of which all things stand, the source of all existence, the ultimate reality that grounds "the structure of being." To say God exists, therefore, is to subject God to the greater totality of being, the whole of reality in which God would only be a part. This god would not be God.

Tillich was not the first theologian to deny God's existence in the name of God's ultimacy and majesty. Friedrich Schleiermacher, Søren Kierkegaard, and Martin Kähler, all of whom influenced Tillich, were likewise critical of reducing God to a being. Unlike these men, however, Tillich was a theologian of the twentieth century which meant he also had to consider unfathomable atrocities when thinking about the nature of God, including the Holocaust of the Jews in his native Germany. A non-interventionist God (i.e., a God who does not directly intervene from heaven like Zeus in the affairs human beings and the events of history) would not be responsible for causing or preventing such atrocities. This gave Tillich's doctrine of God enormous appeal.

The doctrine of God as being-itself provided a morally credible way for affirming the reality of God in view of the Holocaust. It likewise offered a portrait of God compatible with contemporary science which (we recall) was of primary importance to Tillich given his desire to reach people who were "modern in culture and secular in sensibility" (Kelsey, op. cit., p. 87). This is the God, as the Jesuit theologian and scientist George Coyne puts it more recently, who "lets the world be what it will be in all its continuous evolution. He does not intervene, but rather *sustains, allows, participates, loves*" ("Like the Universe, Our Mission Must Evolve: Reflections of a Jesuit

Scientist," *Conversations on Jesuit Higher Education*, Vol. 40, Article 22, p. 42; italics mine). Yet the meaning of being-itself still eludes our grasp. What does it signify? Might it suggest, as some critics of Tillich's view contend, that God is ultimately the lifeless foundation of all things? For an answer we turn to specific discussion regarding the inherent dynamics of being-itself and its everyday confirmation in what Tillich calls the courage to be.

CHAPTER SEVEN

COURAGE

Tillich's view that human courage somehow reveals the inner-dynamics of God undeniably constitutes one of the most provocative claims made by a theologian in the history of Christian thought. Often when people think of divine revelation they might imagine spectacular supernatural events—fire that comes down from heaven or a voice that booms from beyond the clouds. While Tillich provides his own theory regarding revelatory experiences of the divine that appear in classical religion, he also offers a more subtle understanding of how God discloses Godself to people in everyday life. God, he says, "appears" to individuals not as a being "out there" but in the most personal and intimate of ways—in subtle moments of grace where the separation of "life from life" is overcome as well as in moments of deep courage where an individual takes a form of nonbeing (death, meaninglessness, or life-denying guilt) into himself and confronts it, saying "yes" to life in spite of the threat in question. This is an understanding of the divine presence that becomes manifest to human beings as the power of being, one that empowers them to "choose life," as Deuteronomy 30:19 puts it, in spite of existential anxiety.

However provocative, Tillich's view of courage and its relation to God also raises questions, two of which he directly identifies in the final chapter of *The Courage to Be*. "How," he asks, "is the courage to be rooted in being-itself, and how must we understand being-itself in light of the courage to be" (*CTB*, op. cit., p. 156)? What, in other words, is the connection between God and the phenomenon of courage, and what does the courage to be as we experience it within ourselves tell us about God? For an answer we turn once more to Tillich's view of God as being-itself: If God is a process whereby being overcomes nonbeing eternally, the victory of which continuously generates the "stuff" of the material universe, then what we have in Tillich's doctrine of God marks a rehearsal in eternity that people play out in their daily lives. Whenever a person faces and overcomes a threat to the fullness of her being, she echoes in a fragmentary and incomplete way what occurs definitively and completely in God. To clarify what this means the present chapter begins by defining being and nonbeing (as Tillich understands them) as well as how the victory of being over nonbeing in God constitutes the condition for the possibility of all existing or actual being. It concludes by examining how the same victory of being over nonbeing in God can be reflected in the lives of individuals, a supreme example of which appears in the "resurrection" of Jesus *before* he died.

Our first step toward defining being-itself is not an easy one. We have to determine the origin of being! Where does it come from? While answers obviously vary, most fit the mold of what the philosopher Aristotle calls efficient causality. A specific agent in the past (e.g., God), some other finite cause (as in the "big bang"), or a combination of both whirls the universe into being. This form of causality explains the historical origin of being by postulating the existence of someone or something in the past that brought being out of nothing (*creatio ex nihilo*) and set the sequence of cause and effect in motion. Unfortunately, efficient causality becomes problematic theologically if one rejects (as Tillich does) the idea of God as a being. It also fails to explain what theologians refer to as *creatio continua*, namely, the idea of material creation as an *ongoing or continuous activity*, because it reduces the origin of being to an event in the past without explaining what sustains it in the present.

The notion of creation as an ongoing act implies a different form of causation, the kind Aristotle defines as material causality. If efficient causality explains the origin of something as the result of another agent or finite cause, material causality points to the "stuff" or the material of an object as its cause. Consider how a chair comes into being. The efficient cause would be the person who builds it. The material cause would be the substance or material out of which it is made. With regard to the origin of finite or material being in general, Tillich rejects efficient causality (as noted) because it reduces God to a link (albeit the first one) in the chain of cause and effect, making God by implication finite. Thinking of God in terms of material causality, on the other hand, avoids this pitfall. The "stuff" of being has its source in being-itself which, like the rays of the sun, continuously radiates outward, giving being to all beings each and every moment they have being. Obviously we are not the source of our own being; it comes each second from another source. The source from which it originates (for Tillich) is being-itself, the material cause of all finite being.

What, then, is being-itself? Is it a lifeless substance or an immovable ground, as some of Tillich's critics suggest? Many interpreters of Tillich (including the author of the present work) answer in the negative. As distinct from the category of substance, Tillich maintains that being-itself contains within it an element of resistance, the overcoming of which implies dynamism or movement. At the same time the overcoming occurs beyond the temporal process so that we can only speak of it as analogous to an event in time: something "happens" in God, something like what happens when a person faces and overcomes a threat to her vitality. The meaning with respect to God partially differs from the way we use it regarding ourselves because God as being-itself is not a being in time subject to time.

Tillich names the resistance in God that God overcomes "nonbeing." O'Neill identifies Tillich's characterization of the relationship between being and nonbeing in God perfectly:

> Being-itself, or the 'power of being-itself', is the power of God, discernable [sic] in the Creation of God, the revelation of Jesus the Christ, and the Spiritual Presence within human life and history. However, as

revealed power, being-itself comprises two impulses: 'being', the impulse to create, to reveal, to be present; and 'non-being', the necessary limitation of that infinite potential. This duality of being and non-being is *the* ontological concept of Tillich's theology and forms the basis of his doctrine of God and his anthropology [i.e., his view or interpretation of human nature] (O'Neill, op. cit., p. 52, italics original).

This explanation helps us to see how nonbeing functions and why it is necessary in the creation of the material world. It has the task of curbing unlimited being (*ST*, vol. 1, op. cit., p. 189). Without nonbeing there would be no distinction to being, no differentiation between objects or various beings. Nonbeing makes finite being possible. In God being overcomes nonbeing, the limiting factor or negation of itself eternally, which is why Tillich refers to God as "the eternal process in which separation is posited and overcome by reunion" (*Ibid.*, p. 242). Here "separation" refers to the limitation of being in God which God confronts and then incorporates into Godself. This resolves the opposition between being and nonbeing in God, the achievement of which results in the production of finite being.

Perhaps a comparison (however imperfect) will help. Imagine a watch with only one hand that starts at the position of nine-o'clock. Each second it moves until it reaches three o'clock. There it stops because of an obstruction. With each tick the hand vibrates but goes nowhere. Suddenly the obstruction gives way. The hand, in turn, boldly proceeds as it circles the perimeter of the watch again. This process recurs indefinitely. The hand represents being. In each cycle, as it were, being (the clock hand) faces and overcomes nonbeing (the resistance at three-o'clock), generating time as well as material creation. One could say that the process always happens and has already happened, even though the point is the same: victory over nonbeing (where being, going outward, unlike, at this point, the hand on a clock, takes nonbeing or the obstruction into itself) eternally results in the production of temporal being. Each pulse of being, each moment of life, presupposes this conquest of being over nonbeing at the heart of all finite reality.

The victory of being (the impulse to create or the "yes" to life) over nonbeing (the impulse to limit or the "no" to life) makes up what Tillich symbolically calls the "life" in God. Since Tillich defines life as "the process in which potential being becomes actual being," life as we experience it can only be applied symbolically or analogously to divine reality (*Ibid*). God must transcend the split between potentiality (what one ought to be) and actuality (what one is) that comprises all human life; otherwise, God would need healing since the tension between "possibility and fulfillment" in God would be unresolved. Tillich writes, "The divine life inescapably unites possibility with fulfillment. Neither side threatens the other, nor is there a threat of disruption" (*Ibid.*, p. 247). To suggest differently, Tillich concludes, raises the nonsensical and "religiously offensive" question of whether God, like us, would require reconciliation and healing. This would make little sense, Tillich says. How can God, the source of healing, be in need of healing? In contrast to human beings, God achieves within God the perfect balance between being and nonbeing definitively. The name for this stability is being-itself.

Tillich's basic understanding of the conflict and resolution between being and nonbeing in God should be clear. "As being-itself," O'Neill explains, "God constitutes the power of being and nonbeing for human existence as well as for Godself. What is balanced in God, however, is unbalanced in humanity. Under the 'conditions of existence' the polarity of being and nonbeing creates conflict in human existence" (O'Neill, op. cit., p. 58). O'Neill's encapsulation of what comprises being-itself helps us understand both the origin of being as well as the source of evil in the world. Nonbeing functions to limit being, thereby making finite being with all its diversity and differentiation possible. This is good. Under the conditions of existence, however, the negating power of limitation can result in conflict and destruction which (at its extreme) explains the origin of evil in the world. Evil has its root in God as nonbeing even though God has conquered nonbeing eternally and neutralized it within Godself. God is not evil, but the potential for evil (nonbeing) is in God.

Tillich's understanding of nonbeing draws on a long conceptual lineage that includes the philosopher Friedrich Schelling as well as the Lutheran mystic Jacob Boehme, all of whom contend that nonbeing not only delimits being, making the existence of finite forms possible; it also gives being its energy and dynamism. Even God or being-itself necessarily contains or "embraces" nonbeing, as noted. Tillich writes, "Nonbeing makes God a living God. Without the No [nonbeing] he has to overcome in himself and in his creature, the divine Yes [being] to himself would be lifeless. There would be no revelation of the ground of being, there would be no life" (CTB, op. cit., p.180). Yet unlike God, who conquers nonbeing eternally and in the process continually generates the being of the cosmos, the finite objects and organisms that derive their being from being-itself (i.e., everything that exists) only resist nonbeing partially and temporarily. They all eventually perish. Nonbeing sets finite being on fire, giving life, energy, and movement to that which it simultaneously consumes, breaks down, and destroys.

The good news is that we derive the power at least partially to resist nonbeing from being-itself. Whenever we overcome nonbeing through an act of courageous self-affirmation (i.e., by saying "yes" to life in the face of existential anxiety) we echo in time what God does eternally. This is why Tillich sees the phenomenon of courage or the ability to affirm oneself in the face of nonbeing as the "key" that unlocks the mystery of being-itself. We will return shortly to Tillich's understanding of this courage as it appears in human life. For now we can at least see why human beings encounter nonbeing. The force that propels being forward simultaneously swallows it up. Because we are estranged from God, we are susceptible to the disintegrating power of nonbeing in a way that the source of being—being-itself—is not. Such disintegration can affect us physically (as in death) as well as spiritually (as in the loss of meaning which results in despair).

How, then, do we get from the stability of being-itself to the disruption of being and nonbeing in human existence? To answer this question Tillich utilizes the story of the fall of Adam in Genesis to describe the migration from being in its potential state (in nearness to God as symbolized by Adam before the fall) to being in its actual state (in separation from God as symbolized by Adam after the fall). This requires some unpacking. Recall first that to exist means to stand out or emerge from something else. The "something else" in question is our essential nature or, as Taylor puts it, "what we are in essence or ought to be" (Taylor, op. cit., p. 144). It corresponds, as noted, to "Adam before the fall," who, in succumbing to the desire to eat of the tree of the knowledge of good and evil (Genesis 3:6), transitions from undecided potentiality or "dreaming innocence," as Tillich calls it, to "finite freedom" and self-conscious awareness. This is the state in which human beings are "thrown," as the philosopher Heidegger says: they can raise questions about themselves, the world, and their source because they stand out from being in its undifferentiated form. They exist. Their emergence from the matrix of divine being makes possible self-conscious awareness which the opening of their eyes symbolizes (Genesis 3:7). Now they are separate and distinct from God.

The finite freedom which is generated by the transition from essence to existence also makes sin possible. Drawing on a long theological tradition, Tillich depicts sin not simply as an act of wrongdoing but a condition. "The state of existence is the state of estrangement," he writes. "Man is estranged from the ground of his being, from other beings, and from himself.

The transition from essence to existence results in personal guilt and universal tragedy" (*ST*, vol. 2, op. cit., p. 44). The term "estrangement," as Tillich points out, comes from Hegel; it also surfaces in Calvin's description of sin in *The Institutes of the Christian Religion*. Other theologians do not use the term explicitly, but the implicit equation of sin and separation or estrangement from God appears in Luther and Augustine as well as the writings of the Apostle Paul who, Tillich observes, typically speaks of "Sin" in the singular and casts it as "a quasi-personal power which ruled this world" (*Ibid.*, p. 46).

This is not to say, of course, that sins do not emerge from sin. They do. Like a disease, the condition of separation from God yields certain symptoms which appear in three basic forms: *hubris*, unbelief, and concupiscence. Livingston defines the meaning of these terms in Tillich's theology as follows:

> Unbelief is the turning away from or separation of the will from the will of God, whereas *hubris* is the other side of unbelief, viz, the turning in on oneself and elevating the self to the center of one's world. Concupiscence is the "unlimited desire to draw the whole of reality into one's self." This is seen in all aspects of human life (Livingston, op. cit., p. 146).

The obvious trouble with these "marks of estrangement" is that they cut a person off from other human beings and God, the source of being; the self, in turn, ceases to be itself authentically in relation to others, a deficit which results in loneliness, meaninglessness, and ultimately despair (the "sickness unto death," as Kierkegaard calls it, which he defines as the desire to rid oneself of oneself).

The situation of "finite freedom" and with it the estrangement that Adam's expulsion from the Garden of Eden symbolizes helps us understand, finally, why as human beings we find ourselves longing for "something more." We are incomplete. We know intuitively (Tillich says) that there is something greater from which we have been separated. We "mourn," as does all of nature, for a "lost good" (*SF*, op. cit., p. 76f). We desire reunion and with it, healing. "In the state of estrangement," Livingston explains, "the individual seeks salvation (*salvus* meaning 'healthy' or 'whole'). But because our very existence is estranged, we cannot save ourselves. Despite this fact, we continue to seek salvation on our own" (Livingston, op. cit., p. 146). We are, in short, driven beyond ourselves. We seek a new state of things, a new being. In our finitude, a finitude which makes our freedom actual, we long for redemption, for healing, for reunion with our true selves, others, and God. When healing occurs we have what Tillich identifies as "essentialization," a term he borrows from Schelling. The triad of essence, existence, and essentialization correspond, in turn, to humanity in its pre-fallen state, humanity in its fallen state, and humanity in its restored state—the Kingdom of God (O'Neill, op. cit., p. 32).

How, then, does a person address the problem of estrangement and begin the process of healing (i.e., reconciliation with God)? Tillich answers by arguing that human beings require the courage to be, the power to face the anxieties endemic to estranged (i.e., fallen) existence. In a television interview toward the end of his life Tillich explained why courage became a central topic for him theologically. It was, he says, at least partially a response to the pervasive sense of disappointment people seemed to experience in the aftermath of the Second World War. The world "looked darker" due to the split that occurred between Eastern and Western powers. A sacred void had opened. Emptiness became a major threat, especially with the advent of the Cold War and the haunting prospect of nuclear annihilation, which Tillich could demonstrate through an analysis of the dominant cultural forms (i.e., art, philosophy, and literature) that appeared at the time. Drawing on the symbols and resources of the Bible as well as the Christian tradition, the "courage to be" became Tillich's response to the predicament. The courage to be, however, has a special meaning. It is "not the courage of the soldier," he explains, "but the courage of the human being who feels all the riddles and all the meaninglessness of life and who nevertheless is able to say 'yes' to life."

What does it mean to say "yes" to life? It means confronting the anxiety that comes with adversity for the sake of fully affirming one's being. Tillich provides the example of Socrates for the sake of illustration. According to the story (as Plato tells it), Socrates' countrymen sentenced him to death for supposedly "corrupting" the minds of the youth who gathered around him. The charge is obviously unjust as the story unfolds, but Socrates fails to receive a fair trial and so he must face the inevitability of his impending death. In the story Plato focuses much of his attention on the arguments Socrates makes for the immortality of the soul, but what matters (as Tillich sees it) is the disposition behind them—namely, "the courage to take one's death into one's self affirmation . . . the courage to die is the test of the courage to be. A self-affirmation which omits taking the affirmation of one's death into itself tries to escape the test of courage, the facing of nonbeing in the most radical way" (*CTB*, op. cit., p. 169). Socrates, of course, passes the test. In spite of his imminent death (which occurs at the end of the story) he says "yes" to life in an incredible instance of the courage to be.

The thrust of this example points to a decision virtually every individual faces at some point in life: one can either face the threat of nonbeing courageously, whether it appears in the form of death, meaninglessness, or life-denying guilt, or one can succumb to the anxiety produced by the threat of nonbeing, diminishing the vitality of one's being, giving up, and saying "no" to life in the process. Examples abound. A young woman finds herself up against the threat of nonbeing in its ultimate form (death) when she learns she has cancer. She can face the prospect of her death directly and say "yes" to her life or she can lose the battle to nonbeing by submitting to her anxiety and letting it overtake her in which case, to use the language of the philosopher Epicurus, her soul dies before the cancer takes the life from her body. A widower, to offer another example, experiences emptiness and the threat of a meaningless existence after the death of his wife and the loss of her companionship. He can acknowledge the emptiness and take it into himself while seeking newness of life or he can buckle under its power and live a life of diminished vitality. He can say "no" to his life with his being. This is the (sometimes unimaginably) difficult struggle of ordinary human beings against the threat of nonbeing in its various forms.

The most important form of the courage to be, at least for our purposes, involves its appearance specifically in one's relation to the transcendent, to God. This is the kind of courage, one synonymous with what Tillich calls "absolute faith" (which we will explain below), that is necessary for facing the anxiety over meaning and its loss so ubiquitous in the modern age. Whether such courage exists is a question Tillich asks with urgency in the last chapter of *The Courage to Be*: "Is there a courage which can conquer the anxiety of meaninglessness and doubt? Or in other words, can the faith which accepts acceptance resist the power of nonbeing in its most radical form" (*Ibid.*, p. 174)? Tillich answers in the affirmative. There is a form of faith that can co-exist with meaninglessness and doubt. It has three components, all of which presuppose an honest acceptance of meaninglessness as the only way to proceed.

The first component or "element" of Tillich's answer involves recognizing the presence of the power of being within oneself as one confronts the threat. The power of being, we recall, is the presence of God within us, a power that becomes noticeably manifest when we resist nonbeing in whatever form. This power is primary. It comes before nonbeing which implies that meaning precedes meaninglessness (nonbeing in its spiritual form). *Meaningfulness*, in other words, reflects reality at its ground and depth (i.e., the true state of things) whereas *meaninglessness* constitutes a threat to meaning in the state of estrangement. We participate in the power of being through absolute faith, therefore, when we acknowledge the threat as a threat even in the state of despair. The second component of absolute faith is similar to the first. Tillich writes, "The second element in absolute faith is the dependence of the experience of nonbeing on the experience of being and the dependence of meaninglessness on the experience of meaning. Even in the state of despair one has enough being to make despair possible" (*Ibid.*, p. 177).

The third and final component of absolute faith involves accepting one's own acceptance by a power greater than oneself (namely, God). Here we must pause: What does it mean to accept one's own acceptance? Tillich answers the question briefly in his book, *The Irrelevance and Relevance of the Christian Message*. There exists within all of us, he says, a "continuous repression of disgust with ourselves" (*IR*, op. cit., p. 54). The "acceptance of the unacceptable" marks, in turn, Tillich's way of translating divine grace into language that is meaningful to modern people. "From psychoanalysis," he writes, "I have learned that the unacceptable must first be accepted and only then can be transformed" (*Ibid.*, p. 55). In our acceptance we receive the power of being to confront meaninglessness as "a gift which precedes or determines the character of every act of will" (*ST*, vol. 2, op. cit., p. 125). We do not earn the power to resist nonbeing. We receive it by grace. A reality greater than we are has accepted us by bestowing us with the power of being to confront nonbeing. To use more conventional, religious terminology: God works through us by empowering us to resist threats against the full affirmation of our being. God does so purely as an expression of God's love.

Conscious of the power of being within us, a power not our own, we can confront nonbeing in the form of meaninglessness. Tillich writes:

Of course, in the state of despair there is nobody and nothing that accepts. But there is the power of acceptance itself which is experienced. Meaninglessness, as long as it is experienced, includes an experience of the "power of acceptance". To accept this power of acceptance consciously is the religious answer of absolute faith, of a faith which has been deprived by doubt of any concrete content, which nevertheless is faith and the source of the most paradoxical manifestation of the courage to be (*CTB*, op. cit., p. 177).

When Tillich talks about the deprivation by doubt of any "concrete content," he refers to the demise of a particular concept of God. This is the kind of meaninglessness where a person finds herself alone in a seemingly godless universe, one where the God of ordinary theism who exists "out there" has met its demise under the hammer of men like Nietzsche. But, as we have seen, this God was never truly God according to Tillich. A new God, the "God above God," emerges in its place without concrete content. It is pure divinity, the unconditioned, the God to whom one relates in the posture of absolute faith which, as Tillich explains, "says Yes to being without seeing anything concrete which could conquer the nonbeing in fate and death" (*Ibid.*, p. 189). This is what Kierkegaard describes as being out over 70,000 fathoms of water, sustained (in Tillich's language) by "that which is greater than you, and the name of which you do not know" (*SF*, op. cit., p. 162). This is faith in its absolute, most daring sense.

Such faith, we learn, is not available on its own. It is not, Tillich says, "a place where one can live, it is without a name, a church, a cult, a theology" (*CTB*, op. cit., p. 189). Instead, its posture lies at the depth of explicitly religious faith. Through the symbol for God one transcends the ordinary idea of God by saying "Yes" to being, a "Yes-saying" that ultimately leaves behind "God" for the sake of God. As J. Heywood Thomas, an early commentator on Tillich's theology, puts it: "Absolute faith requires the idea of a God above God, the God who becomes manifest when the God of theism has died" (J. Heywood Thomas, *Paul Tillich*, John Knox Press, 1966, p. 14). In contrast to subsequent death of God theologians of the late 1960s, Tillich does not maintain that God as such has died. Instead, a misconception of God has died. The idea of God as a being "out there" is not only "bad theology," he says; it is no longer palatable as a belief to people who are "modern in culture and secular in sensibility," to cite once more Kelsey's phrase. That God is dead.

We can see, finally, why Tillich defines absolute faith in terms of the courage to be. He writes:

> Faith is the state of being grasped by the power of being-itself. The courage to be is an expression of faith and what "faith" means must be understood through the courage to be. We have defined courage as the self-affirmation of being in spite of nonbeing. The power of this self-affirmation is the power of being which is effective in every act of courage. Faith is the experience of this power (*CTB*, op. cit., p. 172).

Faith, in short, is not an opinion or a belief; it is a posture, one that says "Yes" to life in spite of life's insecurities and uncertainties. The appearance in human life of such faith and with it the courage to be brings Tillich to a powerful conclusion. "Not arguments," he observes, "but the courage to be reveals the true nature of being-itself. By affirming our being we participate in the self-affirmation of being-itself. There are no valid arguments for the 'existence' of God, but there are acts of courage in which we affirm the power of being, whether we know it or not" (*Ibid.*, p. 181).

Perhaps the greatest expression of the courage to be in the Christian faith appears in the life of Jesus himself and the "resurrection" he experienced *before* he died. The true meaning of resurrection, as the theologians Rebecca Parker and Joanne Carlson Brown put it, is "radical courage." They write:

Fullness of life is attained in moments of decision for . . . faithfulness and integrity. When the threat of death is refused and the choice is made for justice, radical love, and liberation, the power of death is overthrown. . . . Resurrection means that death is overcome in those precise instances when human beings choose life, refusing the threat of death. Jesus climbed out of the grave in the Garden of Gethsemane when he refused to abandon his commitment to the truth even though his enemies threatened him with death. On Good Friday, the Resurrected One was Crucified (*Christianity, Patriarchy, and Abuse*, Joanne Carlson Brown and Carole Bohn, eds., Pilgrim Press, 1989, p. 28).

Jesus' life bears powerful witness to the courage to be. Tillich insists, moreover, that in Christ something decisive has happened, something of perennial relevance for all human beings, especially those who find themselves riddled by doubt and despair. To Jesus' story and its consequences according to Tillich we now turn.

CHAPTER EIGHT

CHRIST

What would it look like to live a life as the human being God intended? Can we imagine an existence in which the
"marks of estrangement" do not appear, one where an individual enjoys union with his truest and deepest self, with others
and God? We can, Tillich suggests, if we turn to the portrait of
Jesus as the Christ in the New Testament. There we see, as in
a work of art, "a human life that maintained the union [with
himself, others and God] in spite of everything that drove
him into separation" (*ET*, op. cit., p. 96). This achievement
provides the answer to the quest for healing and wholeness
inherent to being human, one that gives Jesus as the Christ
enduring relevance to humanity in all times and in all places. In
him, Tillich says, we have the appearance of "essential humanity" and with it the "new being" in an actual person. Through
him, Tillich adds, we can receive the power of the new being
or "the power in him which has conquered existential estrangement in himself and in everyone who participates in him"
(*ST*, vol. 2., op. cit., p.125). We can be reconciled (however
fragmentarily) to ourselves, our neighbor and God if we are
"grasped" by the "reality which radiates through Jesus' image,
as that was remembered by the disciples when they received it"
(*IR*, op. cit., p. 53).

Tillich's understanding of who Jesus was (his Christology)
and how Jesus saves (his soteriology) pit him against popular
Christian opinion, at least as he sees it. He rejects, for example,
any "Jesusology" in which people depict Christ "as a God walk-
ing on earth" because it undercuts Jesus' full humanity and
with it his complete "participation in existential estrangement"
(*ST*, vol. 2, op. cit., p. 133). This is a problem because it denies

Christ's *actual* victory over demonic forces that tempted him "to make himself in his finitude absolute without the self-sacrificial death" he undergoes on the cross (*IR*, op. cit., p. 53). It also turns him into an idol. Without Jesus' self-negation Christians lack the foundation necessary for criticizing absolutism since otherwise Jesus takes the place of God. When this happens the cross in principle gives way to the Swastika as Jesus eclipses the "true ultimate" by becoming the object of demonic devotion.

The New Testament, however, tells a different story. It offers (as Tillich reads it) the portrait of a human life in which the conflicts of existence have been overcome, and it does so in a way that can "mediate" healing to those who are "grasped" by its power. This means that salvation for Tillich is a *present reality* available through Christ to human beings (see 2 Corinthians 6:2), not simply something waiting for them after they die. What, then, is this healing power that saves people by stripping them of their old self and clothing them with a new one, as Colossians 3:9 puts it? How does Tillich define it, and how does the answer he gives invite his readers to consider the meaning of salvation in a totally different light, not to mention evangelism and who or what constitutes the Christian church? For answers to these questions we now consider Tillich's Christology as the definitive and final answer to the search for fulfillment endemic to the human condition.

Tillich presents his Christology in a number of different works, most notably in the second volume of *Systematic Theology*, in *The Irrelevance and Relevance of the Christian Message*, and in a powerful sermon titled "The New Being." In the first and second of these texts he addresses at the outset the problems raised by critical scholarship concerning the existence of Jesus and whether the stories about him that we have in the New Testament are historically reliable. He maintains that the "Christ-event" consists of both "fact" and "reception." Something happened. While we cannot with certainty establish all the details as they surface in the Gospel accounts (an endeavor that Tillich, following Martin Kähler, held to be important but not decisive for confirming the truth of Christianity and its message), we can infer that the reality "shining" through his image transformed men and women who were close to him as well as those in subsequent generations who accessed his image through the biblical record. This is important. It changes the terms of the debate by showing that what matters for faith revolves entirely around the being of Jesus and whether through him people experienced transformation.

Tillich clarifies his point in *The Irrelevance and Relevance of the Christian Message*:

> Christ, in strict theological terms, would not be the Christ without the church, that is, the community that received him. And the church would not be the church without the Christ on whom the church is based. Now this means that Christianity is not based on an idea or a set of symbols. They are there. They are used. But the church is based on something that has happened in time and space—the appearance of a man who is called Jesus who is received as the expected Christ (*IR*, op. cit., pp. 46-47).

Consider the point closely. The event in question (i.e., the "something that has happened") has little to do with what Jesus may or may not have done, whether he fed 5,000 people by the Sea of Galilee, or where he was actually born. Historical research can only establish with regard to such details "more or less probable results," none of which can serve as the basis for acceptance or rejection of the Christian message (*PTTB*, op. cit., p. 216). What matters is the "truth" of Jesus' being, the new being or new reality that appears in him, and whether this reality has an affect upon those who came into contact with it. Based on Jesus' reception we can say, therefore, that the New Testament "presupposes" the appearance of the new being in history, but its real importance lies in the impact it has, as

Taylor points out, on the "present faith of the community of Christians" (Taylor, op. cit., p. 25).

What, then, is the new being? How does Tillich describe it? Following the Apostle Paul, Tillich depicts Christ as the second Adam or the new creation. (Adam in Hebrew simply means "humanity.") The "new humanity," he says, has appeared in Jesus. For Tillich, however, this is not exactly a return to Adam in the state of "dreaming innocence" before the fall. Instead, the new being "points directly to the cleavage between essential and existential being—and is the restorative principle of this whole theological system. The new being is new in so far as it is the undistorted manifestation of essential being within and under the conditions of existence" (*ST*, vol. 2, op. cit., p. 119). This requires explanation, and fortunately Tillich provides it. The new being is new for two reasons: "it is new in contrast to the merely potential character of essential being; and it is new over and against the estranged character of existential being. It is actual, conquering the estrangement of actual existence" (*Ibid*). Estrangement, we recall, constitutes separation from one's true being or essential self, from others, and from God. Under the conditions of estrangement, Tillich argues, Christ maintains unity with all three, manifesting in the process the "new being" in history.

Tillich's view of Christ as "essential humanity" under the conditions of existence fits within a framework that finds expression in thinkers ranging from Augustine to Luther. It has three parts: human beings (along with the rest of God's creation) are 1) essentially good, 2) actually fallen, and in need of healing which 3) comes through the appearance of the "last Adam" (1 Corinthians 15:45) or the new being in the midst of estrangement, Jesus the Christ (*TC*, op. cit., pp. 118-119). While no "traces of estrangement" appear between Jesus and God, "tensions" exist within his being, anxieties which he must take into himself and overcome. He is also tempted to make himself absolute. This is because he is truly human. He fully participates in existence which brings with it "uncertainty in judgment, risks of error, the limits of power, and the vicissitudes of life" (*ST*, vol. 2., op cit., p. 131)—all of which the biblical record confirms. Christians do not follow Jesus because he knows everything, Tillich argues. They are grasped, as Paul and the disciples were, by "the power in him which has conquered existential estrangement in himself and everyone who participates in him" (*Ibid.*, p. 125). They are grasped by the truth of his being, a truth which becomes manifest in "the uniqueness of his relation to God" and in the way he relates to others (*Ibid.*, p. 127).

As an illustration consider the story of the man who calls Jesus "good teacher" and then asks him what he must do to inherit eternal life (Mark 10:17-22). Jesus responds first by denying the goodness of anyone but God alone, a powerful act of self-negation that avoids the temptation he faces in his vocation as the Messiah to take the place of God. After Jesus suggests the man follow the Ten Commandments and learns that he has done so, the text gives us insight into what Tillich would call the truth of Jesus' being: "Jesus, looking at him, *loved him* and said: 'You lack one thing: go, sell what you own, and give the money to the poor, and you will have treasure in heaven; then come, follow me" (10:21; italics mine). The love Jesus has for the man (however challenging his advice!) as well as for the poor gives us insight into the union that exists between himself and others. We see the same unbroken union appear in Jesus' relation to God, even in the moment of his greatest separation from God while on the cross where, in agony, he still cries out to God in abandonment.

Tillich calls the unity Jesus maintains with God in the midst of separation from God paradoxical. He writes:

> The paradoxical character of his being consists in the fact that, although he has only finite freedom under the conditions of time and space, he is not estranged from the ground of his being. There are no traces of

unbelief, namely, the removal of his personal center from the divine center which is the subject of his infinite concern. Even in the extreme situation of despair about his messianic work, he cries to his God who has forsaken him. In the same way the biblical picture shows no trace of hubris or self-elevation in spite of his awareness of his messianic vocation. . . . Nor is there any trace of concupiscence in the picture. This point is stressed in the story of the temptation in the desert. Here the desires for food, acknowledgment, and unlimited power are used by Satan as the possible weak spots in the Christ. As the Messiah, he could fulfill these desires. But then he would have been demonic and would have ceased to be the Christ (*Ibid.*, p. 126).

What we have, in short, is the portrait of one who overcame the conflicts of existence, defeating estrangement in himself and maintaining unity with the divine. "Into this unity," Tillich writes, "he accepts the negativities of existence without removing them" (*Ibid.*, p. 135). This includes even the anxiety over having to die which occurs shortly before his execution. This is the courage to be in relation to God.

Tillich identifies the courage to be as a central component of Jesus' "permanent unity" with God. He writes, "The conquest of existential estrangement in the New Being, which is the being of Christ, does not remove finitude and anxiety, ambiguity and tragedy; but it does have the character of taking the negativities of existence into unbroken unity with God" (*Ibid.*, p. 134). Jesus as the bearer of the New Being, in other words, incorporates nonbeing into himself and his relation to God. Only by fully taking on suffering and death, Tillich argues, "could he participate completely in existence and conquer every force of estrangement which tried to dissolve his unity with God" (*Ibid.*, p. 123). The risk, of course, is failure—the victory of anxiety over the power of being in him would have disrupted his unity with God and closed him off to other human beings. But in a supreme expression of absolute faith that says "Yes" to God and life even as the threat of "No" takes his life away from him, Jesus becomes for Tillich the "highest human religious possibility," expressing as he does "the highest form of self-affirmation" in relation to the divine (*IR*, op. cit., p. 52).

The danger of being the "highest human religious possibility," of course, is that it draws all the attention to Jesus himself. This makes him the object of a potentially demonic faith. The cross achieves its final significance, therefore, insofar as it definitively negates him as the object of worship, something he had been doing himself throughout his encounters with other people during his ministry. In the portrait of Jesus as the Christ we discover that "the highest human religious possibility is assumed and annulled at the same time" (Paul Tillich, *The Interpretation of History*, Charles Scribner's Sons, 1936, p. 27). The power of the new being, in turn, radiates through him. By grace we receive the power of the new being as a gift in moments where we overcome the split between our true selves and our actual selves, between our neighbor and ourselves, and finally between ourselves and the source of our being, God. The Christian religion has no exclusive purchase when it comes to the appearance of the new being, but the church has a special task and calling to witness to its appearance in Jesus as the Christ in the hope that those who encounter it will be "grasped" and healed.

What, then, does all this mean for evangelism—for spreading the Word? Tillich makes it clear that the message of the Christian faith concerns the appearance of the "new creation" in Jesus the Christ. "We want only to communicate to [others]," he writes, "an experience we have had that here and there in the world and now and then in ourselves is a New Creation, usually hidden, but sometimes manifest, and certainly manifest in Jesus who is called the Christ" (*ET*, op. cit., p. 93). This new creation, Tillich continues, should be our "ultimate concern" and our "infinite passion." Nothing else in Christianity or any other religion matters except the healing that comes with the new state of things where the old disruptions in being have been healed and the fulfillment human beings seek has been (at least partially) realized.

What, finally, does even a partial realization of the new creation in history look like in the life of an individual human being? Tillich provides us with a glimpse toward the end of his sermon, "The New Being." He writes:

> Where the New Reality appears, one feels united with God, the ground and meaning of one's existence. One has what has been called the love of one's destiny, and what, today, we might call the courage to take upon ourselves our own anxiety. Then one has the astonishing experience of feeling reunited with one's self, not in pride and false self-satisfaction, but in a deep self-acceptance. One accepts one's self as something which is eternally important, eternally loved, eternally accepted. The disgust at one's self, the hatred of one's self has disappeared. There is a center, a direction, a meaning for life. All healing—bodily and mental— creates this union of one's self with one's self. Where there is real healing, *there* is the New Being, the New Creation (*Ibid.*, p. 96; italics original).

The biblical picture of Jesus as the Christ, the "anointed one" by God who bears within himself the "new creation," is the answer to the quest for fulfillment as it appears in an actual human being under the conditions of existence. Such an answer gives the Christian church the responsibility to confess and pronounce that "the reunion of man to man" has been realized, that all are one in Christ, as Paul says in Galatians 3:28. This, Tillich observes as racial tensions continued to escalate in mid-twentieth century America, constitutes the appearance of the New Reality in history—"where one is grasped by a human face as human" even though one must overcome the differences of gender, national identity, ethnicity, age, and "all the other innumerable causes of separation" (*Ibid*).

Obviously, Tillich remarks, the church can and does fail in its responsibility to bear and proclaim the new reality that is manifest in Christ. It too stands under the judgment of the cross. That said, in the portrait of Christ the Christian church possesses a unique "vantage point" from which to name and raise to conscious awareness the appearance of the new being in human life. In its witness to the undistorted appearance of this reality in the image and being of Jesus, moreover, the church makes it available to people in and beyond its walls. Tillich writes:

> Without expression or manifestation everything remains merely potential and does not become actual. Thus, everything I have said about Christianity must have a manifestation to be real. I said "No Christ without the church," which means Jesus could not become manifest as the bearer of the new being without those who receive him as such. The expression of this reception is manifold. It is there in the life of the church, in its symbols of thought and action (*IR*, op. cit., p. 59).

That the church exists, Tillich adds, reflects the human situation of estrangement. The sacred does not reside in a specific building, exclusively among a particular community, or in a segment of reality; it lies at the depth of all reality. Yet on this side of God's kingdom the church is necessary to help make the presence of the new reality available to people. That is its mission and task.

Under the cross the church also has the responsibility to preach "the Crucified who cried to God who remained his God after the God of confidence had left him in the darkness of doubt and meaninglessness" (*CTB*, op. cit., p. 188). Even when Jesus felt abandoned by God Jesus maintained his faith (as evident in the fact that he cries out *to God* just before he dies); now, however, his faith reaches beyond the God of ordinary theism who exists "out there" and fixes our problems by intervention. This claim more than any reveals Tillich's creative attempt to correlate the content of the Christian faith with the modern predicament of meaninglessness. Imagine the possibility! Could it be that the God who did not answer Jesus is the same God who had become silent in the experience of Tillich's contemporaries? Could this be the God of ordinary theism that Tillich says must die so that the "God above God" can appear in its wake? If so, then the absolute faith of Christ on the cross, a faith that reaches through doubt and the demise of a lesser God to the God above God, to being-itself, likewise reaches across nearly twenty centuries as the ultimate expression of the courage which takes doubt and meaninglessness into itself while still saying "Yes" to "something more" by the power of the *new being made manifest in Jesus the Christ.*

The possibility that God as the power of being in us orients us to God draws out a final observation regarding a theological commitment that runs through the entirety of Tillich's work (noted as well in previous chapters): "Only God can reunite the estranged with himself" (*DF*, op. cit., p. 134). While Tillich distanced himself in America from the institutional Lutheran Church, perhaps in part due to the fear (justified or not) of being too parochial, his conviction that the faith which grasps and turns us toward the infinite comes from the infinite itself reflects his debt to Lutheran Protestantism. This tradition informs his stance on a variety of theological topics, from sin understood as a "corruption" of existence to the affirmation of God's actual presence in the midst of such corruption. Tillich acknowledges the influence directly: "I, myself, belong to Lutheranism by birth, education, religious experience, and theological reflection. . . . The substance of my religion is and remains Lutheran" (*IH*, op. cit., p. 54). Throughout the final years of his life, however, Tillich found himself speaking to many people who had no affiliation with a church, Lutheran or otherwise. This raises an important question: Must one belong to a Christian community to be spiritual or religious? Is membership a prerequisite for encountering the new being?

We can piece together Tillich's likely answer by noting the following. First, the community, whose charge is to bear the "spiritual presence" in history, does not always coincide with religious institutions. Second, as Tillich implies in his 1957 essay for *The Saturday Evening Post* and states explicitly in the opening remarks of *The Irrelevance and Relevance of the Christian Message*, going to church does not necessarily make one "religious." At the same time, however, he observes that the community of faith gives faith its language, its "concrete content." "Only as a member of such a community," he writes, "can man have a content for his ultimate concern. Only in a community of language can man actualize his faith" (*DF*, op. cit., p. 27). Even the person who exists apart from the community of faith and calls herself "spiritual but not religious" has to draw upon the language of a faith community and tradition to form, shape, or understand the basis of her religious experience or "awareness" of the unconditioned, as Tillich would put it. Religious experience does not arise in a vacuum: "the act of faith, like every act in man's spiritual life, is dependent on language and therefore on community" (*Ibid*). We can distance ourselves from a particular community of faith or think of our faith as a purely private matter, yet we must still rely on the language of such communities to construct and understand the spiritual dimension of our lives. In that sense at least, faith cannot exist apart from community.

Whether one identifies with a specific religious tradition or not, we all speak from a particular point of view. We all have a bias, and Tillich is no exception. That said, he provides a remarkable illustration of how a theologian can generously consider, and in some cases incorporate, divergent points of view as he works out his own. We see this especially in his attitude toward the great critics of the Christian faith, including Nietzsche and Freud. While Tillich certainly has critics too, we can admire him for embodying an intellectual spirit of openness and hospitality toward those with whom a person of faith might ordinarily disagree. Criticism remains, however, and so we turn our focus from Tillich's Christology and his view of the church to questions his theology raises by way of conclusion.

CONCLUSION

In the academic discipline of theology more dissertations in America have been written on Tillich than perhaps any other Christian intellectual. His influence was pervasive, particularly given his wide range of interest in areas outside of theology, including art, architecture, politics, and philosophy. In psychology Rollo May, who was a student and friend of Tillich's, appropriated many of his ideas. Martin Luther King, who wrote his dissertation on Tillich's doctrine of God and partook in semi-frequent written correspondence with both Tillich and Reinhold Niebuhr, also drew greatly on his theology. In his famous "Letter from a Birmingham Jail," for example, King depicted segregation in Tillichian terms as the quintessential expression of sin as separation, one that epitomizes what Tillich describes as the universally "tragic" condition of human beings in the state of estrangement from one another, themselves, and God. In the latter part of the twentieth century Tillich has been regarded as an important forerunner to ecological theology (H. Paul Santmire) and religious pluralism (Paul Knitter) as well.

Next to his appropriation by male authors, a variety of women in theology have also found Tillich's ideas congenial. His position regarding the inescapably symbolic language for God, one that he partially accepted by the second volume of his *Systematic Theology* even in reference to being-itself, inspired feminist theologians like Sallie McFague to challenge the idolatrous character of male metaphors for God when people take them literally. Of equal (if not greater) influence among emerging feminist theologians was Tillich's view of the courage to be which Mary Daly drew upon as the basis for resisting the patriarchal oppression of women and with it the denial of their full humanity. The fight for women's liberation that emerged in the late 1960s shortly after Tillich died found at least one theological source for the empowerment of women in Tillich's call to people to affirm their being in spite of the threat of nonbeing.

Into the twenty-first century theologians continue to utilize and develop other aspects of Tillich's work, especially his method of correlation, which Taylor considers to be "one of his most influential notions in twentieth-century theology" (Taylor, op. cit., p. 22). Often they do so in ways both appreciative and critical. In *Face of the Deep: A Theology of Becoming*, for instance, Catherine Keller simultaneously affirms and denies Tillich's perspective on courage. Discussing the faith that lures one deeper and deeper into divine mystery, she writes: "Faith as trustful courage is an endless process. I am of course indebted to the spirit if not the ontology of Paul Tillich's classic redefinition of faith in terms of courage, in *The Courage to Be*" (Catherine Keller, *Face of the Deep*, Routledge, 2003, p. 293). Keller's rejection of Tillich's ontology discloses one of the most common problems people have with his theology, namely, his understanding of reality at its depth and ground as "being-itself." This "problem" merits our attention as we consider just a few of the specific difficulties people have raised in response to Tillich's understanding of God.

One of the biggest difficulties critics have with Tillich's identification of God as being-itself concerns its priority over other symbols for divine reality. Is being-itself ultimately more adequate than other terms in pointing to the nature of God? Can it do so in a way that borders on a direct and literal description of God's nature? For his part Tillich would probably maintain the need to utilize a variety of symbols in conjunction with the "power of being" or the "ground of being" to point to different facets of being-itself. But being-itself, he might add, helps give force to a basic intuition concerning the majesty and grandeur of God, a God who resists objectification. "This

God," Tillich says, "will evade you. You can never fix this God. Hence the prohibition to name God, since a name is something you can grasp, something which tries to 'define' or make finite" (*IR*, op. cit., p. 60). Such an observation has considerable precedent in the Jewish and Christian traditions. The language of being-itself belongs to a mighty stream of religious thought that guards against the reduction of the divine to something in the realm of the finite. It corrects what the Tillich scholar Frederick Parrella identifies as the "the fatal flaw in Western philosophy and theology" from Tillich's perspective, namely, "its objectification of God" (*Paul Tillich: A New Catholic Assessment*, Frederick Parrella and Raymond Bulman, eds., The Liturgical Press, 1994, p. 252).

Yet, as critics point out, Tillich's equation of God with being-itself presents another problem. It places him in a trajectory of classical orthodoxy that stuffs God into an attic of being, one that cuts God off from the movement and flow of life in the house of time below. The theologian Keith Ward explains:

> When you realise the immense difference between the classical and popular views of God, you realise, perhaps to your surprise, that the classical view is nearer to the seemingly very radical views of God who is not a particular cause or personal agent in the world, who is not a being among other beings at all. So when conservative Christians attack views like those of the twentieth century theologian Paul Tillich for saying that God is not a person, but is 'Being-itself', the depth and power of being, they are in fact attacking the classical Christian doctrine of God (Keith Ward, *God: A Guide for the Perplexed*, Oneworld, 2002, p. 144).

The trouble with the orthodox or classical portrait of God that Tillich supposedly endorses has become increasingly apparent since the Protestant Reformation: it protects God from objectification and the mess of finitude, but it does so by severing the relationship between God and God's creatures. God is not a person or a being. God is the timeless depth of being totally unaffected by the temporal process. As such, critics wonder, *can God hear our prayers* or respond to us in meaningful, personal ways?

Denying God's capacity to hear prayers directly presents a major stumbling block for Jews and Christians. Livingston articulates the problem nicely: "Tillich's conception of God as 'Being-itself' has raised further questions as to whether he can maintain the biblical conception of a 'personal' God, and this has helped to spark an important debate about the Christian doctrine of God in the latter decades of the twentieth century" (Livingston, op. cit., p. 153). Briefly, critics ask, can an individual pray in a meaningful way to a God beyond personhood? Is not a "personal" God necessary to hear our prayers? Once again Tillich challenges us to think about how we view God. Are our prayers to "Him" no more than merely a conversation between two people? If not, must we simply abandon prayer or can we rethink it? How, in short, might we understand prayer in light of Tillich's doctrine of God?

In the Christian tradition proponents of classical theism, including Martin Luther (to some extent) as well as John Calvin, have argued that the point of prayer is not to change God in terms of God's relation to us; the point of prayer is to change us and our disposition in relation to God. After all, God resides outside the temporal process which means God cannot change. "He" sees all things at once, as Augustine argues, and does not experience duration or process as we do. In prayer the task, therefore, is to align one's temporal will with God's unchanging will (Calvin), to become mindful of the "daily bread" that God constantly provides whether we ask for it or not (Luther), or to raise oneself up to the eternal (Augustine and Tillich). All of these answers assume or imply that the point of prayer is to change our disposition in relation to God. This view of prayer also helps us understand Jesus' claim that God knows our prayers before we ask him (Matthew 6:8).

Seeing prayer as a disposition instead of a dialogue has a long history in the Christian tradition, one that suggests an affinity especially between Tillich's perspective and certain forms of Catholic (i.e., contemplative)spirituality. It has merit. This may not be the only way of reading Tillich, however. Robison James of the North American Paul Tillich Society, for example, sees potential in Tillich's theology for a more dialogical form of prayer, one that stresses the encounter of God in "transpersonal" terms as an "eternal thou" or "you" instead of impersonal terms (which we likewise discussed in chapter six). The same may be said for reading Tillich's doctrine of God, as Ward does, simply as another expression of the "classical view." While Tillich insists that God as being-itself resides outside of time, paradoxically he stresses the closeness between God and world so much that some commentators think he sometimes departs from classical theism by verging on pantheism. Even Taylor, who appears to be sympathetic to Tillich's theology, wonders if the criticism of ordinary theism "led him to risk tracing out God's transcendence so deep in the fabric of existence (at times, even in the abyss) that the meaning of 'transcendence' was stretched beyond recognition" (Taylor, op. cit., p. 23).

How, then, might Tillich respond more fully to the difficulties we have raised? Does the language of being-itself for God make God too impersonal? Can God truly hear our prayers, and does the equation of God with being-itself border too closely on pantheism, the idea that ultimately no difference exists between God and the universe/world? Let us consider a brief answer to each of these questions here.

First, remember the threefold dialectic in Tillich's theology of pre-fallen or essential being, fallen existence, and the healing process of "essentialization" which reunites our existence with its essence. Usually critics who charge Tillich with pantheism (the position again that all is divine or that no distinction exists between God and the world) ignore the paradox in estrangement that we participate in being-itself but *stand out from it* and our essential being at the same time. History has as its final aim the Kingdom of God, which symbolizes the convergence of God and world (see Revelation 21:1-2), but in actuality these two realities remain distinct. On this matter Tillich is once again decidedly classical. Each stage of the triad of essence, existence and essentialization in his theology, as O'Neill tells us, corresponds "to a person of the Trinity, or a manifestation of the 'power of being-itself': God creates perfect human essence; the Christ redeems fallen human existence; and the Spiritual Presence guides the essentialization, or reconciliation, of historical, human existence with its essence" (O'Neill, op. cit., p. 32). Full and final convergence between God and the world, though the aim of history, lies beyond it. Tillich accordingly evades the charge of pantheism, even if his language sometimes suggests otherwise.

What about the opposite charge, then, that Tillich's God remains too removed from the temporal process as the timeless depth of being-itself? Is God, perhaps as Catherine Keller and other process theologians often read Tillich, a lifeless ground or frozen foundation beneath time who can neither feel the joys of God's creatures nor participate in their sorrows? Here we can see how Tillich actually departs from the classical view in spite of Ward's characterization: The resistance in God of nonbeing and its overcoming compel Tillich (albeit symbolically) to speak of God as "the eternal process in which separation is posited and overcome by reunion" (*ST*, vol. 1, op. cit., p. 242). There is a dynamic component within God, one that the classical view rejects, even though the "process" (for Tillich) achieves resolution somehow apart from time. Unlike his classical forbears, moreover, Tillich can affirm that God "suffers" at least analogously to God's creation: God may not be a being who directly feels or responds to us, but in the conflict being has with nonbeing and its overcoming we see a version of the cross and resurrection in the heart of being-itself. No classical theist of antiquity would say that. God does not suffer, according to the classical view. God "exists" beyond the passions in and as the motionless waters of the eternal.

Tillich's departure from the classical view, however slight, places his doctrine of God "on the boundary" (a favorite Tillichian phrase) between viewing God as an eternal stillness completely detached from time and the inner-worldly God of someone like Hegel who plunks God in time and makes God contingent on the people and events of history. Navigating between these two perspectives compels Tillich to inject process into the realm of timelessness; being-itself somehow includes movement. But this is a problem. Do not the words "eternal" and "process" contradict each other? Does not a process imply duration which requires time? Before we answer, we should consider a final observation: Tillich ultimately distinguishes the eternal from the infinite. The infinite, he says, is merely the negation of time or the opposite of time; it is bound to time conceptually. The eternal, by contrast, comprises the infinite and the finite while transcending both. The infinite and the finite are somehow *in* God. Does this help us make sense of why "movement" in terms analogous to our experience of movement and process might be in God even though God is not in time?

If we can affirm somehow that God takes the finite into God while simultaneously transcending time then we have in Tillich's theology what we might call a nuanced version of classical theism, one that might help us make sense of what Tillich means when he claims that people do not simply continue to exist after they die in a heaven of endless duration; instead, they are reunited with the eternal. He writes, "When we 'return to eternity' we do not return. We do not continue our existence in time and space—not even on heavenly meadows—but we are reunited from the eternal ground from which we came and to which we go" (*IR*, op. cit., p. 59; see Romans 11:36). And so Tillich leaves us with a question: Can the eternal incorporate time into itself without becoming what it incorporates? Maybe it can! Maybe the eternal is not the opposite of time but above time in a way that includes a dimension of time in itself.

Trying to imagine how we might incorporate time into a realm beyond time (which boggles the mind) leads us to a final question, one that will close the chapter. Why not simply reverse Tillich's thinking to resolve the problems we have discussed? Instead of trying to stuff time into eternity, why not open the floodgates of eternity and release the waters of being-itself *completely* into time? This approach appears in radical forms of kenotic theology (kenotic refers here to the self-emptying of divine reality into history) as well as in Hegel's philosophy. Tillich rejected kenosis (at least in its Hegelian form) ultimately for this reason: If God is subject to the conflicts of existence that we experience in time, then God (like us) would require healing. God would therefore not be God. "The message of reconciliation is not that God needs to be reconciled," Tillich insists. "How could He be? Since He is the source and power of reconciliation, who could reconcile Him" (*ET*, op. cit., p. 94)? But what if God is working out God's own salvation in the course of history as a process, one that *brings with it* our healing as well? Must God be resolved within Godself outside of time to be the source of healing? Could not God heal others through God's own "self-saving"?

Such an answer, which appeared in the controversial "death of God" theology shortly before Tillich died, was one that he explicitly repudiated. Any talk of God as a process or agent in history he considered "blasphemous," again because it supposedly subjects God to the broader structure of reality. If God needs healing like we do, the reasoning goes, then God is not God. Yet what if, as process theologians like Keller also wonder, "structure" implies a kind of rigidity that fails to approximate the dynamic fluidity and variation of reality at its most basic level? What if the basis of all existence is a *moving* ground, a groundless ground, a dance and sway of energy that exhibits certain patterns but lacks in permanent stability? What if the "religiously offensive" understanding of God as a partner in the voyage toward harmony and greater complexity in history more closely approximates reality? These are the questions we must pose as we read a great theologian like Paul Tillich, a theologian whose system of thought is so rich and vast that perhaps hints and suggestions within it might lead us to new answers that even he could not have imagined.

AFTERTHOUGHTS

Probably the greatest tragedy with regard to Tillich's thought has been that, outside of academic circles, few today know about his work. My hope is that this introduction to his life and thought might, at least in some small way, remedy the problem—especially in a context where the extremes of religious fundamentalism and nihilism dominate the way people see the world and with it, God. Tillich's perspective offers us another way, one that incorporates reason and doubt in the service of faith. While he wrote in a time and for an audience different (at least in some ways) from ours, the German-American theologian's manner of addressing faith-related issues might be just what we need as we confront those of our own.

For readers interested in learning more about Tillich's life and thought beyond the present volume, a number of books may be of interest. The biographical work of Wilhelm and Marion Pauck (*Paul Tillich: His Life and Thought*) has no equal in the literature. That said, Rollo May's *Paulus* provides a nice sketch of Tillich's life from the view of a friend and student. It also offers a helpful counter-perspective to the biography written by Tillich's wife, Hannah, *From Time to Time*. Hannah's biography recounts the open marriage she had with her husband. I have intentionally avoided discussing this aspect of Tillich's personal life in the present introduction, in part because I believe it to be an unnecessary stumbling block and not relevant for appreciating or understanding his writings, but should you, the reader, be interested I invite you to consider all three of the above-mentioned perspectives and judge for yourself.

With regard to Tillich's writings the best way of encountering them directly for the first time is to begin with the sermons.

These provide a wonderful entry into Tillich's thought-world. They appear in three collections: *The Shaking of the Foundations, The Eternal Now,* and *The New Being,* all of which I have cited in the present volume. *The Irrelevance and Relevance of the Christian Message* (including the wonderful introduction by Durwood Foster, a former student of Tillich's) as well as *Dynamics of Faith* would be ideal for readers interested in more elaborate yet still accessible avenues into Tillich's perspective. More technical, but still worth the reader's time, would be *The Courage to Be* as well as the three volumes of Tillich's *Systematic Theology.* A nice primer containing a sampling of these texts as well as others by Tillich appears in F. Forrester Church's *The Essential Tillich,* which was a gift I received from members of Augustana Lutheran Church in St. James, Minnesota, during my days as a student pastor. This text helped me considerably as I tried to make sense of Tillich and is one I recommend accordingly to others new to his thought. A companion workbook accompanying this volume, suitable especially for congregational study, is also available through Lutheran University Press.

Today the internet can also be a useful place to locate information about Tillich. Unfortunately, as I stated in an earlier chapter, a number of websites contain misleading information about Tillich by fundamentalist critics who do not accurately grasp his theology. Probably the best and most reliable place to start if you want to learn more about Tillich online, therefore, is the website of The North American Paul Tillich Society (www.napts.org). There you will find a number of links to books and articles by Tillich as well as those about Tillich written by trustworthy and reputable authors, some of whom have spent their lives studying his work. Whether, finally, you choose to access Tillich's thought through the internet or in books, my hope is that you will find yourself rewarded as I have been. Tillich's theology offers an invitation to rethink *what matters most* in a new and potentially transformative way.

ACKNOWLEDGMENTS

I would like to thank those who have shared with me a love for Tillich's theology, especially my former students at Pacific Lutheran University as well as my current students at Seattle University and Matteo Ricci College, along with my faculty colleagues at both universities.

I am also grateful for mentors who have guided me specifically in my understanding of Tillich, including but not limited to Ted Peters, Frederick Parrella, John H. Elliott, Douglas Oakman, Timothy Lull, Hal Sanks, Don Arthur and members of the North American Paul Tillich Society.

Thank you as well to Albert Anderson and Leonard Flachman for their guidance and patience in the production of this volume.

A special expression of gratitude goes out, finally, to those who helped with the painstaking details of the editing process, especially Olga Peterson, Kelle Rose, and my dear friend, Janet Giddings. Any errors, though unintended, are mine.

INDEX

Dynamics of Faith 8, 12, 26, 42, 43, 44, 47, 51, 53, 54, 56, 59, 62, 64, 66, 69, 74, 75, 110, 111, 123

Easterbrook, Gregg 14
Eckhart, Meister 72
efficient causality 87, 88
efficient cause 88
Einstein, Albert 7, 76
Eliot, George 44
essentialization 94, 117, 118
eternal thou 79, 117
evangelism 102, 107
evil 83, 90, 91, 92
existence of God 37, 71, 74, 76, 80, 81
existentialism 27, 28, 37
extra calvinisticum 19

faith 8, 9, 11, 12, 13, 14, 19, 20, 21, 26, 28, 29, 31, 35, 36, 39, 40, 41, 42, 43, 44, 45, 46, 47, 48, 49, 50, 51, 52, 53, 54, 55, 56, 57, 58, 59, 60, 61, 62, 63, 65, 67, 68, 70, 71, 74, 75, 76, 77, 78, 79, 82, 83, 96, 97, 98, 99, 103, 104, 107, 110, 111, 112, 114, 122
Fascism 30
Feuerbach, Ludwig 44
Foster, Durwood 30, 123
free will 53
Freud, Sigmund 112
Freudian psychoanalysis 28
fundamentalism 14, 69, 122
fundamentalist 30, 31, 123
fundamentalists 30

God 5, 8, 9, 11, 12, 13, 14, 15, 17, 18, 19, 20, 21, 23, 31, 33, 34, 35, 36, 37, 39, 40, 41, 42, 43, 44, 45, 46, 47, 48, 49, 51, 52, 53, 54, 55, 56, 57, 58, 60, 61, 63, 64, 65, 66, 67, 68, 69, 70, 71, 72, 73, 74, 75, 76, 77, 78, 79, 80, 81, 82, 83, 84, 85, 86, 87, 88, 89, 90, 91, 92, 93, 94, 96, 97, 98, 99, 101, 102, 104, 105, 106, 107, 108, 109, 110, 113, 114, 115, 116, 117, 118, 119, 120, 122
God above God 9, 76, 98, 110
God as impersonal 78

God does not exist 71, 74, 75
God exists 71, 72, 74, 75, 84
Gomes, Peter 38
grace 34, 49, 52, 53, 61, 79, 83, 86, 97, 107

Haught, John 46
heaven 18, 73, 79, 84, 86, 105, 119
Hegel, G. F. W. 8, 21, 93, 119, 120
Heidegger, Martin 21, 27, 71, 92
hell 34
Holy Spirit 83
Hoover, J. Edgar 30
hubris 93, 106
hubris, unbelief, and concupiscence 93

idol 23, 39, 62, 102
idolatrous faith 51, 53, 58, 61, 62, 68, 70
idolatry 23, 52, 68
immortality of the soul 95
incarnation 19
infra lutheranum 19
Ireneaus 35

James, Robison 117
Jesus 19, 36, 40, 41, 44, 47, 61, 62, 63, 66, 68, 69, 70, 82, 83, 87, 88, 99, 100, 101, 102, 103, 104, 105, 106, 107, 108, 109, 110, 117
Jesus as the Christ 61, 68, 83, 101, 107, 108
Jesus Christ 47, 82
Jesusolatry 69
Jesusology 101
Jesus the Christ 41, 62, 88, 104, 107, 110
Johnson, Elizabeth 72
justification by grace 34
justification through faith 52
justified by grace 49

Kähler, Martin 19, 52, 84, 103
Kaiser Wilhelm II 20, 22
Keller, Catherine 114, 118
Kelsey, David 13, 21, 45, 84, 99
kenotic theology 120
Kierkegaard, Søren 19, 40, 84, 93, 98
King, Martin Luther 113
Knitter, Paul 113

sacred void 27, 94
salvation 19, 29, 48, 49, 82, 94, 102, 120
Santmire, H. Paul 113
Satan 106
Schelling, Friedrich 91, 94
Schleiermacher, Friedrich 50, 81, 84
science 11, 12, 14, 42, 45, 46, 50, 54, 57, 66, 67, 73, 76, 77, 84
scientific 35, 47, 54, 66, 76, 77, 80
Seeberger, Ehrard & Elisabeth 24
self-critical patriotism 52
sign 58, 59
sin 19, 44, 52, 62, 82, 92, 93, 110, 113
social justice 80
Socrates 95
Spiritual Presence 88, 118
spiritual void 28, 33
substance 88, 110
suprapersonal 77, 78
symbol 25, 57, 58, 59, 60, 61, 62, 63, 64, 68, 69, 70, 71, 74, 77, 78, 79, 98
symbol of a personal God 77, 78, 79
symbols and signs 58
Systematic Theology 15, 21, 29, 71, 63, 71, 74, 78, 80, 83, 89, 93, 97, 101, 102, 104, 105, 113, 118, 123

Taylor, Mark K. 18, 23, 27, 83, 92, 104, 114, 117

technical-scientific knowledge 35
Ten Theses 23

The Courage to Be 8, 13, 29, 33, 34, 36, 38, 54, 64, 76, 78, 86, 91, 95, 96, 98, 99, 109, 114, 123
The Irrelevance and Relevance of the Christian Message 29, 30, 97, 102, 103, 111, 123
The New Being 35, 41, 49, 102, 106, 108, 123
Theology of Culture 28, 29, 75, 81, 104
theonomy 15
The Shaking of the Foundations 54, 61, 94, 98, 123
The Socialist Decision 22, 23
Thomas, J. Heywood 98, 99
Tillich, Hannah 24, 122
transpersonal 78, 117
truth 11, 14, 25, 40, 41, 44, 46, 47, 50, 52, 57, 61, 62, 63, 64, 66, 67, 71, 75, 80, 83, 100, 103, 105

ultimate concern 13, 38, 41, 42, 45, 47, 48, 52, 54, 55, 56, 57, 58, 59, 61, 64, 67, 78, 108, 111
unbelief 93, 106

van Buren, Paul 65

Ward, Keith 115, 117, 118
Weaver, Matthew Lon 30
Weber, Max 34
Wittgenstein, Ludwig 65
wrath of God 34

Zeus 75, 84